The Undivided Heart

Reflections, Stories and Scriptures to Evangelise the Heart

Florence J. Joseph

Onwards and Upwards Publishers
Berkeley House, 11 Nightingale Crescent, Leatherhead,
Surrey, KT24 6PD.
www.onwardsandupwards.org

Printed in the UK by 4edge Limited.

ISBN: 978-1-910197-30-1
Typeface: Sabon LT
Graphic design: LM Graphic Design

Passages other than extracts from texts are diary entries, testimonies, stories and reflections drawn from personal sources. Some names have been changed to protect anonymity.

About the Author

Florence studied modern languages, theology and mission, and enthusiastically followed a missions call to Europe and Africa between 1981 and 1998. She has worked with third sector organisations in health and social care, and served in the areas of pastoral leadership, pastoral care and leadership development.

She is a passionate communicator and loves creative writing, walking, quiet evenings with friends and her postage stamp-sized garden. She is also a proud aunt and great-aunt to an ever-expanding family and counts many precious friends as her legacy in the nations. Florence is based in SW London.

To contact the author, please write to:

fjjministries@gmail.com

Endorsement

I was curious from 'Hello'! When I first read the title and strap-line, I sensed I was being invited into a quiet room for a heart-to-heart conversation. Florence has been a friend for many years, and this book is such a clear description of her journey into real and vital intimacy in her walk with Christ. Allowing him to control all the inner recesses of the soul is like learning how to dance in the arms of another – dangerous, delicate, but ultimately delightful!

Doug Williams
Senior Pastor
Emmanuel Christian Centre, Walthamstow

This book is dedicated to Gladys, Faith, Jonathan, Carolyn, Norma, Jennifer and Rosemary, my early teachers. The seeds they planted and watered have produced an abundant harvest. They instilled in me a hunger for God and His word that remains to this day.

Contents

Acknowledgements

In Memoriam: Special thanks go to the late A.F. (Tony) Derrick, who painstakingly worked on the first draft of the book and encouraged me to get it into print. He did not live to see this desire fulfilled.

N. Elly Jansen, OBE (whose lifework has been dedicated to providing therapeutic residential and supported living services worldwide for people with mental ill health) is owed a genuine debt of gratitude. It was her gentle encouragement to look at myself more critically and take greater responsibility for my actions and attitudes towards others that set me on this path.

Lastly, I want to honour posthumously my parents, Christian Jeremiah and Perlina Floretta Joseph, whose lives turned out very differently to what they had originally dreamed. My African-Caribbean heritage, love of life, food, humour and singing are among the precious gifts I inherited from them. May their memory live on!

Preface

This book reflects part of the journey I have been on for the last twenty-five years. It began in the mid-1980s when I was teetering on the edge of collapse. In full-time Christian work at the time, I was beginning to discover how completely out of touch I was with the real issues of my heart. Lack of insight meant that relationships took the major brunt of the fallout of my unhealed state. Healing came gradually as the different elements of personality, unmet needs, desires and inner drives began to coalesce. The hunger to know God and the real 'me' was to become an important key, unlocking doors of the heart that had remained tightly shut since childhood.

"Give me an undivided heart," prayed the Psalmist, "that I may fear your name." (Psalm 86:11b) I found the late Dr. Derek Prince's exegetical comments on this verse helped steer me in the direction I meant to go:

> *Here is the crucial issue; that we have an undivided heart. We can have no conflicting loyalty, no second option. All our springs must be in God; all our expectations must be from Him. I have discovered in the life of faith that the further we go in God, the fewer our options. The way becomes narrower and narrower. Ultimately those who complete the course are those who have found their total satisfaction in God. It is not God plus something; it is God alone. Our heart is undivided when we do not look anywhere but to God for our satisfaction, our peace, our life.*[1]

The theme of the undivided heart, and our journey into whole heartedness, sums up the best part of my life! This small book describes aspects of that journey, from its origins in God, through the broken and damaged places of our hearts, into the love of the Father and our place in His heart. It is an invitation to engage deeply with our own heart issues, and so be better able to communicate with Him and with

---

1 *Through the Psalms with Derek Prince,* DPM-UK, Baldock, United Kingdom, 2005. *http://www.dpmuk.org* Used with permission.

others from a place of understanding, depth and generosity. What happens here affects everything!

The book's teaching is interspersed with anecdotes, poems and stories. The stories are metaphorical and imagined, though relate to some aspect of the writer's experience of transition.

The road to transformation hinges on our willingness to be small again. It is my prayer that together we can rediscover the joy of travelling light, freed to live and love and laugh with God.

Florence J. Joseph

Foreword by Jennifer Rees Larcombe

Having read this book through once I know I now want to go back and read it very slowly, a little at a time over a number of days, to savour each truth and draw out all the treasures.

Just as an example, two phrases that really impacted me were:-

> *His [Jesus'] own heart pursues lovers, worshippers and friends.*
>
> *Repentance is, simply put, my heart saying, 'Lord, I'm wrong, I'm sorry and I'm yours,' and my life turning in His direction. That's when the love affair begins.*

These are the sort of gems that will bear meditation, chewing over through the day and reflecting on at night.

This is a peep into Florence Joseph's own journey of being pursued by Him and embarking on that Love Affair that never ends. To have an undivided heart is one of the deepest longings of everyone who loves Jesus and, though our journeys will be different, we can learn much from the roadmaps travelled by others. This book is just such a roadmap.

I am going to treat this little book as a devotional that I dip into when I am in need of 'food for the journey'. Perhaps you could too...

Jennifer Rees Larcombe
Beauty from Ashes
September 2014

CHAPTER ONE

Heartbeat

Chambers

Normally no bigger than an average fist, the human heart's every beat signals 'I am!' It is the roll-call I have responded to every day of my existence from early foetal life, beating around seventy times a minute, over one hundred thousand times a day, and over two and half billion times in a typical lifespan. Strategically positioned in the human body and representing the centre of life, the classical world understood it to be the seat of the intellect including thinking, memory and imagination, and the ruling part of the soul. Although their knowledge of the physiology of the heart was limited by modern standards, and only partly understood, there was little doubt about the importance of the heart in the functioning of the entire human organism. It was only with anatomical discoveries of the nervous system by Hellenistic physicians in the third century before Christ that the debate began to turn in favour of the brain being the origin of the nerves and the centre of sensation, consciousness, speech and intelligence.

The ancient Hebrew word for heart – *lev* – embraces the concept of 'mind'. Indeed it has no separate idiom. Inasmuch as it essentially defined the seat of emotion (the deepest intentions, feelings) the term also denoted the process of rational thought, imagination and volition. In Hebrew thinking body, heart, mind and spirit were an interconnected whole, none of which could be separated. The heart signifies the central core of the individual, the inner or true self. It is this understanding of the heart as a mechanism of the soul that forms the basis of the thesis of this book.

The heart is an inner sanctuary (or hell) populated with the most private and personal: loves and hates, pleasures and dislikes, appetites and aversions, objects and notions, passions and terrors. The heart is the storehouse of all that I capture, believe and integrate into the self, both good and bad. The private, inner world and the public world of relationships and actions are served by this vast resource. Feed in the positive, and it normally results in wellbeing. Feed in the negative, especially over time, and sickness of mind and body often accumulates.

One proverb from the Bible says:

A heart at peace gives life to the body, but envy rots the bones.[2]

Another advises:

Above all else, guard your heart, for it is the wellspring of life.[3]

They were at 30,000 feet when she began to feel unwell. Within moments, an oxygen mask was clamped on to Annette's pallid face as her body grew suddenly limp. A waiting ambulance greeted airline crew and an anxious family on Spanish soil forty minutes later, and she was swiftly transferred to the medical team for checks. Colour had by then returned to her cheeks. The doctor monitoring her readings asked if she was an athlete. When she replied she was an aerobics instructor, he nodded his head vigorously: 'Strong heart, strong heart.'

My foray into power-walking was initially to lose weight, then to increase cardio-vascular fitness to enable me to run. With an instinctive dislike of the gym, I chose to walk two different circuits around local streets in south-west London to keep me from boredom. A couple of years later the desire to run has worn off. But the outdoors, with its

2 Proverbs 14:30
3 Proverbs 4:23

heat in summer and cold in winter, things to see and people to look at, has got me hooked. And since brisk walking is almost equivalent to a jog with no shock impact on the heart and joints, my metabolism burns calories faster, the weight has fallen off and I am physically happier and healthier.

When it comes to emotional and spiritual heart health, the picture is not so good. The heart, according to the prophet Jeremiah, is desperately sick. It is wayward and deceptive.[4] It has lost its simple love for God and all things good, having bought into the lie that it can decide for itself what is right and wrong. As significant beings individually valued, honoured and bearing the divine image, we were wired to respond to God in privileged partnership with Him in the stewardship of creation and regular audience in His presence. We were created for worship, the language of delight and reverent wonder at a God who is good, great and glorious, whose plans are amazing, and who put it all so dazzlingly together.

The creation narratives provide a straightforward explanation for our wayward condition. Whether we read the narrative as myth or accept it literally, the fallout from our Adamic nature is patently identifiable. Genesis chapter 3 records the serpent's original devious act of rebellion, and the intentional disobedience that severed the loving relationship between God and His son and daughter in that one error of judgement. Rebellious behaviour manifests itself in cold defiance against a known authority. It draws to itself satanic energy, its true source and inspiration. Rebellion is spelled 'rebel lion'. That is what Satan is: a predator. Caged lions may be handled with cautious respect, but a lion on the loose spells utter disaster – especially when disguised as a snake!

Disobedience is a refusal to comply with rules – whether the Ten Commandments or local council by-laws. We've gone through red stop lights. We've turned a blind eye to parking regulations. The only prohibition given early on in our shared human history was to develop the first couple's ability to make right choices within the clear moral framework God had outlined. It was to equip them, not to live by rules

4 Hosea 14:4

and regulations, but to understand the principles and values that make friendship with God work, to know His heart. Once learned, these very rules and principles would usher them into a level of authority and freedom as sons of God[5] that our hearts cannot even begin to imagine, within a magnificent environment untainted by any form or presence of decay. Forever!

Moral independence, rebellion and disobedience are behaviours deeply embedded in our psyche even after we experience regeneration through the new birth and renewal by the Holy Spirit. Thirty years ago I saw this picture of the church being weighed on God's scales. Each scale-pan had the letters C-H under it, and at the top of the scales the characters U-R were emblazoned, spelling C-H-U-R-C-H. What did they mean? The Holy Spirit explained: "The U stands for Unreality and the R for Rebellion." The implication was that the church (for which we were interceding at the time) was shot through with deception and rebellion at its very heart.

The Father's discipline flows out of a profound desire for our safety and wellbeing, and the provision of boundaries is to protect us from real harm. Little did the first couple know what would be unleashed into paradise by way of the synergistic processes of death, or the genetic fingerprinting that would result from it for thousands of generations to come. Disobedience takes us outside of divine protection, resulting in our being 'captured' by whatever is allowed to control our will (that part of us that alone is truly free): whims, substances, habits, people, experiences or destructive ideas – toxic and diffusing the wonderful passion of life we were created for. There needs to be a public warning on every street, as on every packet of cigarettes: "Sin is dangerous for your health"; "Sin kills".

I remember getting lost as a little girl. Disobeying Mum's orders not to leave the school gates, I wandered home with a schoolmate only

---

5 cf. Romans 8:21,23

to have the front door shut in my face. I walked the streets for hours crying, not knowing where I was or where home was. There was a sense of panic, the experience of being alone, the feelings of guilt, fear, helplessness and desperate need for someone to care or to sort things out. These and more feelings summed up my being lost. My older brothers were eventually sent to find me and bring me home to safety.

The party that loves most suffers most when a relationship breaks down. It must have broken the Father's heart to drive His children out of Eden, His and their perfect home; also generations later when He made the final decision to destroy the earth and its inhabitants.

> *The Lord was grieved ... and his heart was filled with pain.*[6]

The story of redemption is that God has paid in Himself the ultimate price for reversing the effects of sin, the bringing of all created life under the penalty of destruction and His legitimate anger. He calls prodigals home. Disobedience has eternal consequences, but the Father's love is greater than the weight of our sin and waywardness. Every beat of His father-heart cries, "I love you! I will always love you." The prophet Jeremiah adjoins, with particular sweetness:

> *I have loved you with an everlasting love; I have drawn you with loving-kindness.*[7]

These are words written from before the foundation of the world in the blood of Messiah. Addressed to a soon-to-be-exiled remnant in Jerusalem, who tacitly refused to absorb the classroom lessons divine discipline sought to teach, it reveals the recalcitrant nature of our hearts, and the longsuffering love of God.

Our proud individualism and agnostic self-belief disguise the fault-line in our collective psyche. Sooner or later, the self-life begins to implode, or unravel. Rebellion towards God typically leads to existential aloneness and spiritual orphan-hood, for the tree of the knowledge of good and evil exposes us to life from the dark side of satanic control. Some people prefer life that way. Yet the very ecosystems on which our lives depend rely on complex, interconnected

---

6 Genesis 6:6
7 Jeremiah 31:3b

links with other organisms, all intricately held together by the God who supplies our every breath. Many would refute that too. Insistence on our ego-driven, self-imposed isolation leads inevitably to the discovery that we are, in fact, pretty powerless in the big scheme of things. When the alternative gods we trust in fail to deliver, we have nowhere to run and few, if any, resources that work.

From before the beginning of time
I AM yours and you are mine,
I HAVE LOVED YOU!
Knit together in the secret place
I pleaded your cause and pleaded your case,
I HAVE LOVED YOU!
When my love you cruelly scorned
And though you pierced me and never mourned,
Even then, I HAVE LOVED YOU!
My love, an everlasting love
From then, until now and for all eternity,
I HAVE LOVED YOU![8]

God sees us as prodigal children. Something of the throbbing pulse at heaven's centre can be felt when we stand close to Him. This love existed before time began in the perfect unity that is the Godhead: Father, Son and Holy Spirit, a community of persons within the singularity of the divine being.

God is One, a being-in-community. Totally sufficient in Himself, there is no lack to be met in Him. Within the unity of the Godhead there is completeness, satisfaction and delight. Mutual love and deep trust exist between all three Persons, who are one in substance although three in operation. Co-eternal and co-equal,

[8] Copyright © Juliette Hutsby, Manchester. Used with permission.

> *the heart and hub of their intimate life together is self-giving, sacrificial love.*[9]

God seeks primarily to win our hearts over, to woo us to Himself, and then to restore us to His original design and release us into our unique destiny as beloved sons and daughters, appropriate to Who He Is[10]. We have no real idea what this will look like! He is intent on bringing us into the fullness and freedom He enjoys as God, so that His heart and ours come into the unity of the Love that holds everything in itself.

O Tree of Calvary
Send your roots deep down
Into my heart.
Gather together the soil of my heart,
          the sands of my fickleness,
The stones of my stubbornness,
The mud of my desires,
Bind them all together,
O Tree of Calvary,
Interlace them with your strong roots,
          entwine them with the network
Of your love.[11]

Door

> *The heart is deceitful above all things and beyond cure. Who can understand it? I the Lord search the heart and examine the mind,*

---

9 Florence Joseph, *Living Light Bible Reflections*, September-November 2009, ©Nationwide Christian Trust, Mulberry House, Chelmsford Road, High Ongar, Essex CM5 9NL. *www.nationwidechristiantrust.com*. Used with permission.

10 Phrase coined by James Jordan, *The Glorious Freedom of Sons*, Fatherheart Ministries, Taupo, New Zealand

11 Chandran Devanesen, India

to reward a man according to his conduct, according to what his deeds deserve.[12]

Although it is not possible to observe what the heart – the seat of the soul – looks like, Jesus taught that the contents of the heart become explicit in human relations and public behaviour, as we see in our text.[13] Put another way, root-and-branch transformation is mandatory before we can truly know the wonder of God's parenthood in our lives, and experience the joy-filled abandon of children.

In the graphic picture from John's Revelation immortalised by Holman Hunt,[14] Jesus stands at our heart's door waiting for a response, seeking nothing less than ownership of the freehold and entire property. Whether our hearts are stone or flesh, hardened or softened, they react to His every approach and hear His every knock. It leaves us without excuse!

What can wash away my sin? Nothing but the blood of Jesus;
What can make me whole again? Nothing but the blood of Jesus.
Oh, precious is the flow that makes me white as snow;
No other fount I know, nothing but the blood of Jesus.[15]

The Lord Jesus described himself as 'the door'[16] to His Jewish contemporaries. This symbolism would not have been lost on them. They understood that Jesus was identifying Himself with Yahweh's gift of salvation and shalom[17], as well as claiming to be the guardian (or Lord) of each life given to Him. We don't have to look any further than

12 Jeremiah 17:9-10
13 Matthew 7:15-17
14 The Light of the World, 1851-6, William Holman Hunt, 1827-1910
15 Words and music: Robert Lowry, 1886 Public Domain
16 John 10:7,9 (NASB, NKJV)
17 A Hebrew word denoting soundness, wholeness, prosperity and wellness at the root of the biblical concept of peace.

Jesus to find God, for He represents Him perfectly and completely,[18] making Him fully visible to the eyes of our heart.

I want to be a child again
I want to see the world through five-year-old eyes
To walk with my Lord wherever He may lead
To put my trust in Him
Make me a child O Lord
Make my song joy
My heart free
My life a dance
A dance of praise to You[19]

More wonderful still is the fact that He comes looking for us, knocking on our heart's door, anxiously pursuing us. Why? It is to bring us to His Father. That is why our older Brother, Jesus, is sent to bring us home and into the joy of His Father's house. This is God's eternal home for us – lost, hurting, fearful humanity. It is a place of love and healing, where masks can be removed and grace appropriated. The kingdom of heaven can be received only by children!

There it was. I strained to hear it. Faint, but just audible above the whistle of the breeze. It was a light sound not unlike the murmur of voices. A skilled musician with the lightest touch was stroking keys in rapid, rhythmic succession so that a cascade of sound fell, a waterfall of soft silver sound. Somewhere on my right it tinkled happily, unseen. It was so soothing. "Come and play!" Play. My mind went back over the years. It stopped short at the doll's bed. Made for the only doll I ever had, and hated. It was cheap and ugly, a present from a visiting Auntie I had never met before and never saw

18 Hebrews 1:3
19 CCLI Song number 306844. Diane Davis Andrew, ©1975 Celebration Used with permission

again. "What kind of a doll is that, with its hard, bald head and limbs of pink, coarse thin plastic?" I despised it, and Auntie. The bed I sat on and broke. No more doll's furniture, and no more dolls. "Who wants dolls, anyway?"

"Come and play!" tinkled the brook, invitingly. I found it hard to respond to its call, caught in the sudden grip of hate that had risen unbidden to the surface of my consciousness. Play? It was the rough and tumble I enjoyed, leaping from chair to chair, building tents over the old settee, wigwams, cowboys and Indians; the wood-smooth banisters we slid down, landing in an occasional heap at the bottom of the stairs. It was the grazed knees from the playground, chalk and skipping rope and limbo dancing under string made from lengths of thin rubber band, and the screams during kiss-chase. Not silly, stupid dolls. I thought about stroking straw-silk tresses and combing long hair, about ensuring dolly was properly dressed and put to bed at the right time, about tea parties and pastel-coloured tea sets in pretty dolls' houses, and I wondered at my vengeful, murderous thoughts.

A hot tear rolled down one cheek, then the other. Slow, small droplets of salted dew gathered pace, dripped off the edge of my face and splashed on to the ground. I hadn't realised before how much I loathed myself, how fully I had buried the child's dreams under the thin veneer of adult needs and adult thinking. Suddenly, in a great surge of pity I gathered the long-forgotten, discarded imaginary doll and cradled it in the crease of my arm. "How lonely you must have felt." Time stood still as tears bathed the dusty plastic frame and reconciled the two individuals. The silent, regular 'plop' could have been a heartbeat. Then, a quickly reconstructed bed and knitted square for blanket, and dolly was laid to rest. It was tough being a girl in a boys' world. But that's the way it had been then.

I felt strangely light as I continued downhill, quite oblivious to my surroundings. It was a breaking twig that finally jolted me back to the present. Startled, my gaze fell and focused. There was the brook! Whereas I could only hear it before, now I could see it, transparent and shiny right to its pebbly bottom. It flowed in easy motion, in a slow figure-hugging waltz. I walked over and bent down low to capture the dance between my fingers. It was ice cold to the touch, clear as crystal. No sediment could be seen, only the brightly coloured stones reposing in their places underwater. These were the groomed spectators, watching while the swirling waters provided entertainment. "Come and play!" I let my fingers play with the tripping current that danced and somersaulted over impassive rocks. We danced together silently until the cold embrace stole over my fingers, and I retracted my hand with reluctance. My eyes followed its antics, while the slow rhythms soothed and lulled my thoughts to rest. The quiet ripples ebbed into stillness and then silence as I walked on and the brook continued its course, away from the direction in which I was headed. It seemed as if, from time to time, echoes of its call were carried on the wind as a reminder to me to cherish and not forget our meeting. As if I could.[20]

Threshold

She lay prostrate on the floor in quiet worship when she saw the Lord pulling something out of her heart, like a long tendril or root. He pulled and kept pulling until she thought it would never stop.

"What is that, Lord?" she asked, perplexed.

"This is a root of un-love and hurt I am pulling out of your heart," He said. "I am giving you My love to love My people with. And remember: they are My people. Pour into them what I am pouring into you."

---

[20] Florence Joseph © 2000

Once he gets past the door, a good salesman is nearly home and dry. But Jesus is no salesman. He comes intentionally to take legal ownership of lives that belong to Him by virtue of His vicarious death on the cross. And what messed-up, broken lives! He is after something infinitely precious to God that reduces everything else to the mere superficial: our hearts, whatever their present condition.

> Greater grace, deeper mercy, wider love, higher ways
> Perfect peace, complete forgiveness...
> All I desire and all I require
> It's all found in you.[21]

This, however, is not a forced entry. Jesus comes with an invitation from His Father. He has so much to share, reveal and do with us, as much as we could hope for or believe – no more, no less. His own heart, you see, pursues lovers, worshippers and friends. This is no textbook relationship but one based on intimacy, disclosure and being face-to-face, where love looks at Love, and in the looking becomes more radiant and fulsome. The threshold is the place where we take the plunge to risk an encounter with the Love of all loves. What makes it so difficult is the fact that we have a distorted view of what God looks like. It is a caricature.

I grew up thinking I had to earn God's love, and I couldn't get it. It took six attempts at asking Jesus into my heart as a child before the penny dropped: He said He would come in the first time. I had been traumatised by the memories of an angry dad who never let us off the hook as kids when we did something wrong, and I simply projected that onto the canvas that was God.

---

[21] Greater Grace by Chris Bowater © copyright 1999 Sovereign Lifestyle Music Ltd. Reproduced by permission *sovereignmusic@aol.com*

So we refuse to dance: "I don't believe in God and all that stuff." "Having made the decision that God cannot be trusted with the things that matter most, I conclude that the only person I can really trust is myself."[22] The caricature sticks, the lies creating an insulating wall of unbelief and rejection around our heart. If the truth be known, much of our lives is a parody of our true selves, the real man or woman of the heart buried under a veneer of projections, defence mechanisms and masks that cover our emotional nakedness. We run from anything that exposes us to ourselves, and to anyone who will tell us who we are, the way we want to hear it. It's as old as the story of Adam and Eve.

The old black coal scuttle, purchased from a friend who was clearing her late mother's property, was cleaned from time to time but led a rather squalid existence. Eventually it travelled with me to my new home, where it sat in a corner and became the dumping ground for unused phone directories. When it looked particularly soiled and grimy one day, I opted to give it a polish. Somewhere from the back of the cupboard emerged a tin of Brasso. Digging out newspapers and two soft dusters with a sigh I began the thankless task of rubbing the bulky object wedged between my knees. A glint of bright pink took me totally off guard. I rubbed harder. Disbelief and then excitement grabbed me as dull black metal yielded to the warmth and glow of rich copper. I squealed with delight when the burnished copper scuttle was finally polished. It was a beautiful thing, buried under the grime of years of neglect, which had suddenly been restored.[23]

---

[22] Beverley Shepherd, *No longer orphans*, Inspiring Women Every Day ©CWR 2010

[23] Florence Joseph, *Living Light Bible Reflections*, September-November 2009, ©Nationwide Christian Trust, Mulberry House, Chelmsford Road, High Ongar, Essex CM5 9NL. *www.nationwidechristiantrust.com.* Used with permission.

Christian belief is a common target for parody. What Jesus Christ presents us with is truth – not religion, dogma or philosophical notions but the truth of who He is, and what we are in the light of Him. The threshold is where we decide what and whom we will believe. It is where we can choose to admit to ourselves and to Him that our survival strategies have been misinformed and are an insult to His love. Repentance is, simply put, my heart saying, "Lord, I'm wrong, I'm sorry and I'm Yours," and my life turning in His direction. That's when the love affair begins.

Hearth

Picture, if you will, the dancing flames of a roaring wood-burning stove on a freezing cold day. The heat is ferocious but measured, behind protective glass. It is a small scale representation of the love Father extends to us.

> *Place me like a seal over your heart, like a seal on your arm; for love is as strong as death, its jealousy unyielding as the grave. It burns like blazing fire, like a mighty flame. Many waters cannot quench love, rivers cannot wash it away. If one were to give all the wealth of his house for love, it would be utterly scorned.*[24]

The beloved, in our text from the beautiful and poetic Song of Songs, seeks a permanent place in her lover's heart. She uses the implacability of death as a metaphor of her lover's passion for her. This love is compared to a mighty fire – consider for a moment the heat required to bring precious silver to its boiling point of around two thousand degrees Celsius – and to many waters. Who can forget the terrifying scenes of the Indian Ocean tsunami in 2004 which claimed just under a quarter of a million lives? Both images speak powerfully of love that is unstoppable in its reach, and unquenchable in its jealous protection of the one it cherishes. It makes a wreckage of any obstacle in its path.

How does this text translate for us? While lonely hearts yearn to be someone's 'significant other', the King of Love has sought us out to love us and to deeply, everlastingly and wholly satisfy our hunger for

---

[24] Song of Solomon 8:6-7

acceptance, belonging and value. Welcomed and appropriated, His love heals the broken places of our hearts as the substance of Who He Is pours into the substance of who we are.[25] It fills the empty places love has not reached. It restores the soul to life and wholeness, and reclaims our private world. He loves us! More precisely, He loves me.

O Love that wilt not let me go,
I rest my weary soul in thee;
I give thee back the life I owe,
That in thy ocean depths its flow
May richer, fuller be.[26]

Why? The simple answer is this:

The Lord did not set his affection on you and choose you because you were more numerous than other peoples, for you were the fewest of all peoples. But it was because the Lord loved you.[27]

In simple words, God can only be to us who He eternally is; and He is love. We will never fully grasp why He loves us. In the *Revelations of Divine Love*, 14th century Julian of Norwich attempts an explanation:

At the same time, our Lord showed me a spiritual vision of his familiar love. I saw that for us he is everything that we find good and comforting. He is our clothing, wrapping us for love, embracing and enclosing us for tender love, so that he can never leave us, being himself everything that is good for us, as I understand it.

In this vision he also showed a little thing, the size of a hazelnut in the palm of my hand, and it was as round as a ball. I looked at it with my mind's eye and thought, 'What can this be?' And the answer came to me, 'It is all that is made.' I wondered how it could

---

25 James Jordab, The Glorious Freedom of Sons, Fatherheart Ministries, Taupo, New Zealand

26 George Matheson, 1882

27 Deuteronomy 7:7-8a

last, for it was so small I thought it might suddenly have disappeared. And the answer in my mind was, 'It lasts and will last for ever because God loves it; and everything exists in the same way by the love of God.'[28]

> You are more beautiful than Solomon
> More precious than his gold
> I made you higher than the angels
> Your beauty yet untold
> Look at the mountains
> Look at the trees
> Look at the birds of the air
> Feel the breeze
> Look at the oceans
> Fathom the seas
> You're more beautiful than these
> Beautiful
> More beautiful to me[29]

My very existence, the fact that I am, is because He eternally loves. I existed mysteriously within His heart before time began. More precious than an infant separated from the womb at birth, He lovingly shaped my substance and released me into the earth to thrive, to become more fully His and more fully me, until I am tenderly gathered back to Him again. Should I choose never to return, He forever relinquishes that precious part of Himself He loved into life.

As fire naturally draws us to itself on a cold day, we are drawn to the heat and light Jesus radiates. His presence produces fire, but not of

---

28 From *REVELATIONS OF DIVINE LOVE* by Julian of Norwich, translated by Elizabeth Spearing, introduction and notes by A. C. Spearing (Penguin Classics, 1998). Translation copyright © Elizabeth Spearing, 1998. Introduction and Notes © A. C. Spearing, 1998, p47. Reproduced by permission of Penguin Books Ltd.

29 The words were taken from the song *Beautiful* which appears on the CD *Father's Love* by John Nuttall, 2007. Used with permission.

the domestic sort. His fire is all-consuming and deadly. As we welcome Christ as Lover of the heart, holy fire comes in at the door.

He will baptise you with the Holy Spirit and with fire.[30]

But who can endure the day of his coming? Who can stand when he appears? For he will be like a refiner's fire or a launderer's soap. He will sit as a refiner and purifier of silver; he will purify the Levites and refine them like gold and silver.[31]

His eyes were like blazing fire. His feet were like bronze glowing in a furnace, and his voice was like the sound of rushing waters. His face was like the sun shining in all its brilliance. When I saw him, I fell at his feet as though dead. Then he placed his right hand on me and said: "Do not be afraid." [32]

And, in the famous words of Elizabeth Barrett Browning:

Earth's crammed with heaven,
And every common bush afire with God;
But only he who sees takes off his shoes –
The rest sit round it and pluck blackberries.[33]

---

30 Matthew 3:11
31 Malachi 3:2-3
32 Revelation 1:15-16
33 Elizabeth Barrett Browning, 1806-1861

CHAPTER TWO

Contractions

I will give them an undivided heart and put a new spirit in them; I will remove from them their heart of stone and give them a heart of flesh. They will be my people, and I will be their God.[34]

Rid yourselves of all the offences you have committed, and get a new heart and a new spirit.[35]

Surrender

It was hard leaving my friends behind. Not people, but old ways of thinking, like comfortable clothes that had stretched and become my shape and fit. They were now tight, unforgiving and had seen better days. There was a definite need to move on, but it was hard to let go. So the tussle began. Did I really have to part with this stuff? I could just squeeze into those leggings... The familiar wardrobe made me realise how much I had changed. I took a mental tour of the experiences that had moulded me over the years, the places I had been, the impact they had left upon me. I couldn't go back. Things had to go.

A new thought pushed its way into my consciousness. It seemed to surface from a place that seldom saw light. Looking down into the deep water of my soul I saw my stern face reflected in shadow. 'Why

[34] Ezekiel 11:19
[35] Ezekiel 18:31

now?' Those two, short words echoed round cold cavern walls, filling my ears with sound as they ricocheted back and forth. 'Why now, now, now?' It was a while before the last echo disappeared and I became conscious again of my face staring back at me. With intense effort I searched within for a response. It seemed an eternity of waiting. Suddenly a glimmer of light appeared, glowing and growing as it approached like a train out of a tunnel. As the light loomed large before me the cavern, the deep water and my stern face got lost in broad daylight. My eyes were adjusting to the sudden brightness when I found myself in wild grass, high as my head, in the company of a tall stranger who stood to my right, his body inclined towards me.

The man appeared friendly. As I took in my surroundings with a glance, the man walked ahead of me, pushing the grasses out of the way with his arms and body. I followed. The tall, dry, pampas-like grass surrounded me on all sides. Only the stranger's presence and our rhythmic movements filled the quiet, relentless plain. We walked on, silently and in file. I had the growing confidence that the man knew where he was going but I was anxious. I wanted to leave this isolated place. Instinctively, as if reading my thoughts he turned, smiled briefly and wordlessly communicated, 'We'll soon be there.' Sure enough, moments later we emerged onto a grassy verge. Open skies and wide, undulating expanses bathed my senses. It was all so spacious and green. My dull eyes feasted on a meal of colour and texture. I was startled as the man spoke for the first time, breaking the silence.

'I am the Way-Maker. I walk people out of the past and into places of growth, helping them transition and manage the process of change. Once on the other side, they are free to walk the new paths and explore new places until these grow too small for them and they are ready for bigger challenges. Then I take them to the next place.' He smiled warmly, and with just a hint of a grin added, 'Have fun.' With a friendly nod, he turned on his heels and walked back into the tall grass from which we had emerged. I watched him go with a

strange sense of sadness mixed with a tinge of excitement. The quiet grass had masked a powerful surge of feelings of vulnerability and loss. Now, in the open, a sudden wild abandon took hold of me and I leapt into the air, punching it with my fists. 'Yes, yes, YES!' I crouched low, touched the meadow grass lovingly, laid out full length under an open heaven, and slept.[36]

The heart of stone – cold, hardened, inflexible and impenetrable – is the legacy of ancestor Adam's free-will decision that has become humanity's default position before God. Outside of His living presence in the heart and providential activity in our lives, we are largely dead to all things spiritual (while remaining fascinated by the supernatural), bound with fears and ungodly beliefs, hard-pushed to maintain any consistent level of integrity in our behaviour and lifestyles, and destitute of the agape[37] love that reaches beyond itself in self-giving service. The apostle Paul is rather more candid:

You were dead in your trespasses and sins.[38]

God's indictment of His covenant people was that His rules were good but their hearts were fickle. The Old Testament prophets yearned for the day when the 'matter of the heart' would be radically reversed.

We are singularly blessed to be living under the generous terms of God's 'new' covenant, now over two thousand years old. Jesus' sacrificial death on the cross was the price paid by the Father for our collective ransom, attested by the divine blood of the innocent Lamb of God. Every curse known to man, every vile act, every form of depravity and wickedness was laid on the one and only, sinless Son of God. His death-defying, hell-busting, devil-destroying, life-releasing resurrection from the dead means that every man, woman and child who desires it has a legal right to heaven's aid, legal access to the throne

---

[36] Florence Joseph © 2000

[37] A Greek word used in the New Testament to describe the sacrificial and unconditional love of God – the highest form of love that exists.

[38] Ephesians 2:1

of God and is legally entitled to call God their Father, 'Abba' and Dad. Love wins. It's that profound.

> Amazing love
> O what sacrifice
> The Son of God given for me
> My debt he pays and my death he dies
> That I might live[39]

It also turns Jewish thinking on its head. No devout worshipper in their right Jewish mind could conceive of approaching the holiest place on earth without utmost fear, the most rigorous self-examination and diligent compliance with the ancient rituals and regulations of centuries of temple worship. For him, unlike his Gentile counterpart, the remission of sins was always identified with blood – the life of an innocent animal offered to a holy God in place, and on behalf, of one who rightly deserved to die.

Max Lucado puts it brilliantly:

> *A Chinese Christian understood this point. Before her baptism, a pastor asked a question to ensure she understood the meaning of the cross. "Did Jesus have any sin?" he inquired. "Yes," she replied. Troubled, he repeated the question. "He had sin," she answered positively. The leader set out to correct her, but she insisted, "He had mine."*
>
> *Though healthy, Jesus took our disease upon himself. Though diseased, we who accept his offer are pronounced healthy. More than pardoned, we are declared innocent. We enter heaven, not with healed hearts, but with his heart. It is as if we have never sinned.*[40]

---

[39] Graham Kendrick, *Amazing Love*, Copyright © 1989 Make Way Music, *www.grahamkendrick.co.uk* International copyright secured. All rights reserved. Used by permission.

[40] Reprinted by permission. *3:16 The Numbers of Hope*, Max Lucado, ©2007, Thomas Nelson Inc., Nashville, Tennessee. All rights reserved.

The gospel always requires a change of heart, course and direction. It starts with true conviction, the admission that we are sinners in need of a Saviour, who need to come home to the Father (viz. a hot shower, clean clothes and food[41]), where forgiveness can be sought and is instantly given. God's love does not recriminate or condemn, nor does it make us feel small and embarrassed. Rather, it is gracious and kind, full of hope and encouragement, patience and empowerment. It is a most wonderful gift, and not a one-off experience. We will find ourselves returning frequently to the Father, owning up to our messes with varying amounts of contrition, at times to be disciplined or grounded. In turning to Him, repentant or hesitantly, we are met with undeserved favour and overwhelming mercy in the form of unconditional acceptance, total forgiveness, bucket-loads of reassurance and a new understanding of our place in His heart as beloved sons and daughters. Any morbid fear on our part is understandable and forgivable. No one may have told us just how good God is, and how all-encompassing and retroactive the forgiveness He gives us. This 'coming home' is essential to our healing, just as opening our heart's door to the Lord Jesus allows the regeneration of the dead places within us. It is a significant step in the right direction when we run to, and not from, the Lord of life.

Megan's dad was the managing director of a legal firm in South Africa, and I recall her telling how as a child she would work her way through the layers of staff and secretaries to get to him. However, once at the boardroom door, her father would stop proceedings, stand up and say, "Gentlemen, my daughter." Tearing round the room she would shake the outstretched hand of every man standing, "Hello, hello, hello," until she got to him: "Dad, can I have some money, please?"

---

41 cf. Luke 15:21-22

Having not had a father to run to, or having a father you would rather not be near, puts some of us at a disadvantage when it comes to experiencing God as a loving Dad. However, the Holy Spirit can heal our hearts, reaching beneath the source of pain to reconnect us with our legitimate, innate hunger for love and belonging.

Sandy was an attractive, articulate, fifty-something Christian woman. An exercise during a retreat I was leading left her so shaken she approached me at lunchtime to talk about it. Each woman had been invited, through the creative use of her imagination, to enter God's throne room in heaven and enjoy Father-daughter time for fifteen minutes. As Sandy got to the throne room door, wild horses wouldn't drag her in. Such was her terror that she called on Jesus for help! Jesus gently coaxed her into the room, legs shaking, inviting her to come to His Father who was just like Him. As she inched her way to several feet from the throne, anxious and nervous, she heard God invite her to sit right next to Him. She shook her head. He slowly stepped down from His throne and, smiling, stretched out His little finger towards hers. She slowly stuck out her little finger, made tentative contact and jumped back, asking the Lord Jesus to take her away. Her legs continued to shake like jelly while several women shared feedback from their time in the throne room before lunch. Sandy expressed shock that, having walked with God for decades, there was distance and aloofness in the way she related as a child to her Father. She also shared that she'd had an abusive dad, and the relationship had not improved much with the years. After prayer ministry that afternoon she returned home and revisited the throne room scene again. To her great comfort she found herself running this time straight into the arms of Father God on His throne.

As new life pours in, there is an informal exchange we enter into at the cross that requires a letting go of the stony heart. Wounds of the past have a way of hardening. Psychological walls get erected as a form of human shield against interlopers. Bitter-root judgements and inner vows bind our hearts in unforgiveness towards ourselves and others, locking us into hurt, anger, hatred and depression. The heart can become an impregnable fortress holding us to ransom, even while grace works from the inside to demolish the walls of fear and mistrust that keep God at arm's length. It makes good sense to call a truce and put up the white flag of surrender.

It is this vital collaboration with the Holy Spirit that determines how deeply the heart is healed, transformed and cleansed to live in the fullness and freedom of the Father's house. The New Testament brings together these two aspects of the work of transformation outlined in our opening passages – one wrought by God, the other provided by us – in Paul's exhortation:

> *Work out your salvation with fear and trembling, for it is God who works in you to will and to do of his good pleasure.*[42]

God is looking to meet us in the broken places: the wounds, memories and shattered dreams that make up the stony heart. We will find Him far nicer and more cognizant of our struggles than we realised. He is interested in who we are, and what makes us tick, rather than whether we simply toe the line.

Loss

The values of God's kingdom are precisely the reverse of those of our culture.

> *Enter through the narrow gate. For wide is the gate and broad is the road that leads to destruction, and many enter through it. But small is the gate and narrow the road that leads to life, and only a few find it.*[43]

The gospel is a revolutionary, counter-cultural message that does not sit comfortably with our post-Christian, politically correct, pluralist and consensual approach to life. Without cost-bearing love,

---

[42] Philippians 2:12
[43] Matthew 7:13-14

radical discipleship and holy living in the power of the Spirit, Christianity is reduced to mere ethics and hot air. How deadly! The cross is the most powerful symbol in the universe of the triumph of holy Love over enmity. It is where God acted decisively in history to rout the demonic principalities that imprison human lives and civilisations until they rot and suffer the eternal death that is their fate. Jesus Christ came to deliver us from the power of sin, death and the destroyer, and to train us to destroy the works of the devil as He did.[44] Jesus is the narrow gate to an extraordinary life – there is no other Saviour, no other remedy for sin, no other legitimate pathway to the Father.

Having said that, the Holy Spirit works within all faiths and cultures to woo and capture the hearts of a lost generation for God's beloved Son, the darling of heaven. The nations are destined to come to His light and the harvest is gathering apace. To enter our Father's house we must abandon the sins and weights[45] that will not – indeed, *cannot* – bow to Christ's Lordship or be transformed by His dynamic working. Identification with the person and message of Jesus Christ will impact our lives in unforeseen ways, some of them costly – but isn't it worth it to be set free from shame and guilt, to know His forgiveness and live a transformed life? To know our Father intimately and joyously and the sheer magnitude of His greatness and glory in the Son constitutes the highest quality of life we can comprehend or experience.[46] The cross of Jesus compels us to let even good things go that become toxic for us.

Joy had nurtured a personal dream of living in the country since her twenties. Wholly dependent on round-the-clock care due to severe brain damage at birth, she lived a quiet but contented life with her parents in London. I can't remember when she began growing shrubs and plants in pots in the hope that one day she

[44] Acts 10:38
[45] Hebrews 12:1
[46] John 17:3

would have her own home and garden but, with her mother's help, she created a beautiful and restful sanctuary. As a compensation claim for medical negligence lasting eight years slowly went through the courts, she occasionally allowed her hopes to rise as she drew mental pictures of her ideal home. It would have a garden, a water butt to collect rainwater, an outside tap, a little greenhouse, wisteria on the wall and, inside the bungalow, a fireplace in the lounge. Joy was not to know that her legal case would founder on a technicality and collapse, leaving Counsel, family and close friends in deep shock. What would her future hold now when her parents were gone? Picking up the pieces of her shattered dreams, she swallowed her tears as her mother sadly admitted, "God must have some other way of providing for you."

He did. Not many years later, a seed thought in the mind of one trustee became a full-blown vision to provide a home for her and her mother as a fitting tribute and recompense for her late father's years of Christian service. Joy was elated. But it would take several years to materialise, and occupied all her waking moments.

It was on holiday, as the group was being challenged whether there were things in their lives God wanted them to lay down, that Joy came to a sudden decision. Taking a fir cone[47] from a pile on the floor, she had it placed at the foot of the cross. Her desire for a home of her own had become too important and all-consuming. With real pain in her heart, she let go of her eleven-year dream.

It was six days after returning from holiday when she got the call. A suitable property had been located; could they come over and view it? A lovely bungalow met her, with a fireplace in the lounge. It had a spacious garden with an outside tap, three water butts and a little greenhouse. There were two garages and

[47] Gathered from the garden to symbolise objects or people to be surrendered to Jesus at the cross.

sheds, and wisteria growing up one of the walls; there was also room for a large bathroom suitable for her needs to be built on to what would be her bedroom. It was all she had dreamed of, and more.

I am not ashamed of the gospel, for it is the power of God for the salvation of everyone who believes: first for the Jew, then for the Gentile.[48]

The simple message of the cross is deeply offensive to our Western, humanist mindsets. For our hearts to thrive in the fertile soil of love and truth, our unregenerate minds also require a thorough cleansing and transformation. The belief systems that govern the way society thinks – through the culture, media, education, entertainment, politics, philosophy, the arts, science and religion – place humanity at the centre of life, not Christ. The cross calls us to depose the self and unmask every idol put in place of God. Dr. Graham tells us bluntly that modern society has become addicted to the 'cult of self' – to ego-driven self-absorption – and that some suggest this may be a defensive reaction to today's depersonalised lifestyles.[49]

The new heart – with the laws of God enshrined within it, coupled with motivation and power to obey – replaces the heart of stone! The new heart enables us to believe who God says He is; to live above the pressure of the rational, mental, intellectual, psychological and social conditioning of our upbringing and to trust, like children, the goodness of God as expressed through His word to us. The Bible introduces us to kingdom thinking and the laws that govern supernatural life in the realm of the Spirit, such as love, blessing, forgiveness, honour, generosity, justice. Through the gate of the new heart we apprehend and are taught by the Spirit of truth. The mind and counsel of God, the 'unsearchable riches of knowledge and wisdom hidden in Christ' that our culture cannot receive or understand – and rejects out of hand –

---

48 Romans 1:16

49 *Storm Warning*, Billy Graham, 1992 and 2010, 174, Thomas Nelson Inc, Nashville, Tennessee

are revealed to us as we worship. We learn to think spiritually, and biblically, to release our grip of man-centred strategies and solutions to our problems, our limited perspectives and our control of life, people and situations. We learn to speak the language of heaven. Anything good we thought we'd brought with us, we might as well let it go. In fact, everything we bring with us from the old heart into the new is destined for an upgrade. The new supersedes the old and makes the old obsolete.[50]

One of the principles of the kingdom of God is that life proceeds from death. It is the law of sowing and reaping with a twist. Everything that is given up for Jesus' sake returns, but not necessarily in the form of its initial investment. It comes back different – metamorphosed and incorruptible, not subject to decay or destruction, because it has taken on new energy and become an integral component of the Family business! The initial small gate we enter in Christ leads to life such as we have never before experienced. And the pain of personal loss is, in part, an initiation into our Father's suffering heart as He looks out over a world writhing and groaning as in the pains of childbirth[51]. The new heart is wired to touch the depths of God's own pain as structural evil and rampant individual sin take their toll of innocent lives, and as human, free-will choice alienates potential sons and daughters from an eternity in heaven in favour of eternal darkness, and a torrid state of everlasting destruction.

She walked up to the cross, spat on it, and said, "God, I have never ever believed in you, and if you were alive I would spit on you because that's all you're worth. If you were real and you allowed me to go through the abuse I've been through, then you are no God that anybody should bother with." She spat on it again, and then she kicked it. She burst into tears and started hitting it, first with her hands and then with a piece of fallen wood from a nearby hedgerow. She was angry and declared, "If

[50] Hebrews 8:13
[51] Romans 8:22

you were alive you wouldn't be able to contain or handle my hatred, but you're not."

Eventually the anger, pain and tears subsided and she stood there sobbing. A voice spoke to her and said, "Take hold of the cross." She nearly jumped out of her skin, partly because she hadn't heard anybody come up behind her, but also because she thought she'd been careful to ensure that there was nobody around to see what she was doing. She turned, but there was nobody there. She was thinking that this was a little weird when she heard the same voice again. The third time she looked around once more to check that no one could see her, and then, feeling rather foolish, she took hold of the cross. The same voice said to her, "Now move the cross." She was quite a substantial lady but she couldn't move the cross at all. Then the voice said, "You cannot move it, because it's immovable. My love for you is immovable. I've been with you through your pain and through the abuse, and I hate what you've been through. I'm not for the abuse; I'm for you. I'm standing here so that you can pour out your anger, pain, hurt and frustration onto me. I will carry it on the cross. My cross is immovable, just as my love is immovable. When you've poured all your anger and hatred on me, I will just say to you that I love you." Within moments she found herself weeping and kneeling in front of the cross, crying out a prayer of acceptance to a God she had never understood to be a God of love.[52]

Travail

The time comes when we must allow the Lord Jesus to bring down the strongholds of our heart, if we are going to walk with Him in any degree of intimacy, for He is a jealous Lover. These have usually been established from our earliest years. They are structures, built to protect

[52] Copyright 2008 by Roy Godwin and Dave Roberts. *The Grace Outpouring* published by David C. Cook. Publisher permission required to reproduce. All rights reserved.

our heart from further pain, that lock the original traumatic events with their negative memories deep in the psyche. Later in adult life, some totally unrelated event replays the forgotten past and stirs up the strongly repressed emotions. We may project the negative feelings associated with key figures from our past on to new authority or parental figures in our lives. Outbursts out of all proportion to the presenting situation can create further pain and misunderstanding for all involved.

Unforgiveness and bitterness, together with the wounds of perceived or actual offence, make it difficult for our hearts to trust and receive love from our Father and other benign sources. We could say much the same for jealousy, fear, disappointment or self-pity. They create an opening for deception to work its havoc, for the Holy Spirit will step back in the absence of truth and honesty. They undermine the words God plants in our hearts, as we rationalise our way out of the need to confront the beliefs and behaviour that unconsciously reinforce the lies we embraced in our formative years. Facing our personal demons is hard work. The Lord Jesus explained to a perplexed group of disciples facing criticism for not complying with the Jewish ritual of hand-washing before taking food:

> *...the things that come out of the mouth come from the heart, and these make a man 'unclean'. For out of the heart come evil thoughts, murder, adultery, sexual immorality, theft, false testimony, slander.*[53]

His assertion that an evil thought in the heart equated with an evil act, even if it was not actualised,[54] raised the integrity bar to new heights.

What is a stronghold? It is any dominant thought-pattern, attitude, behaviour or mindset that becomes a *modus operandi* opposing the rule and reign of God in our lives.

> *For though we live in the world, we do not wage war as the world does. The weapons we fight with are not the weapons of the world. On the contrary, they have divine power to demolish*

[53] Matthew 15:18-19
[54] Matthew 5:27

strongholds. We demolish arguments and every pretension that sets itself up against the knowledge of God, and we take captive every thought to make it obedient to Christ.[55]

The battle for the mind does not cease when we become believers; it intensifies. Our earlier hostility to Christ was predicated on argument: bias and reasoning that defended our entrenched position. This 'fortress mentality' is a deliberate strategy of the powers of darkness to blind the minds of unbelievers to the truth of the gospel and keep us in our lost state. The old, militant mindsets of life 'before Christ' with their deep roots in the subconscious become a means of hijacking the new life of God within our heart and spirit. The late Selwyn Hughes further clarifies this:

Modern psychology tells us that down in the subconscious lie the instincts holding within them the race habits and tendencies. These instincts have gathered up within themselves the race experience which goes all the way back to Adam. They, therefore, have certain leanings, certain drives, which, unrestrained, tend toward evil. In conversion, there is a sweeping out of the conscious mind all that conflicts with the love of Christ and the establishing of his reign there. For weeks after conversion perhaps no conflict ensues, the new life reigns supreme. The instincts of the subconscious are cowed, so to speak, cowed but not converted. They soon demand recognition and expression. They knock at the door of the conscious. The supposed instincts are, as Dr E. Stanley Jones described them, 'like Chinese pirates who hide in the hold of a vessel and then rise up while the ship is on her voyage to try and capture the bridge and with it the ship. A fight ensues.' The issue, then, is this: can the subconscious be converted? Converted, yes. Eradicated, no.[56]

The heart has other enemies, like the distractions the ordinary cares of life bring – and idols. Idols of the heart include anything that competes with the Lord for first place. The wisest monarch of the Old Testament, King Solomon, developed a fetish for beautiful foreign

---

55 2 Corinthians 10:3-5

56 Selwyn Hughes, *A new heart*, Kingsway, East Sussex 1982, 36. Used with permission.

women, and it is recorded that in later life, his love for them displaced his affection for God.

> *As Solomon grew old, his wives turned his heart after other gods, and his heart was not fully devoted to the LORD his God, as the heart of David his father had been. He did not follow the LORD completely. The LORD became angry with Solomon because his heart had turned away from the LORD.*[57]

Solomon held a very special place in God's heart from birth, and was given the name Jedidiah, meaning 'loved by the Lord', as a pseudonym.[58] His wide-ranging literary, oratorical and entrepreneurial talents were the tacit overflow of blessing that rested on him as a loved child, and of the joy of a relationship unmatched in his father's dysfunctional and warring royal household.

The idols his heart followed were foreign gods, alternative forms of worship behind which, I am convinced, masquerade demon powers. What our hearts go after, we worship: pop idols, porn, political power. Lurking behind the public face of private addictions are voracious unclean spirits, happy for us to indulge our cravings while they satiate their bloodlust, like vampires. Once our affections have been stolen, the heart begins inevitably to harden and turn away from its first love, even while it is being imprisoned, defiled and enslaved to its noxious desires. It is not pretty.

The key to freedom lies in repentance, return and renunciation of every stronghold of the stony heart. We are admonished:

> *Do not love the world or anything in the world. For everything in the world – the cravings of sinful man, the lust of his eyes and the boasting of what he has and does – comes not from the Father but from the world. The world and its desires pass away.*[59]

Admittedly, we often do not hate these structures of sin and bondage strongly enough to pay the price for our deliverance. Meanwhile, God waits to be gracious to us. As our need becomes more telling and the oppression intensifies, it wrings a cry from us that our

---

57 1 Kings 11:4,6,9
58 Samuel 12:24-25
59 1 John 2:15-17

Father has been waiting to hear. As with contractions, pain is a fairly good indicator that birth is on the way.

CHAPTER THREE

Enlargement

Blessed are the pure in heart, for they shall see God.[60]

Simplicity

It was Jesus Himself who set the parameters for greatness squarely at the feet of a little child.

> *And he said: "I tell you the truth, unless you change and become like little children, you will never enter the kingdom of heaven. Therefore, whoever humbles himself like this child is the greatest in the kingdom of heaven."* [61]

The gospel writers Mark and Luke place their version of events in the context of a squabble among the disciples as to who was the greatest. Talk about children!

There is something disarming (and scary) about people who are frank and honest. Like the chance interview I caught of an Oprah Winfrey show with Iyanla Vanzant, her 'no-nonsense relationship expert' of the late 1990s. They set the record straight on the rift between the two strong personalities live on air, as Iyanla told the candid story of the loss of her home, marriage, multi-million-dollar book contracts and daughter after a desperate battle with cancer[62]. This

60 Matthew 5:8
61 Matthew 18:2-4
62 Iyanla Vanzant, *Peace from Broken Pieces: How to get through what you're going through,* SmileyBooks, New York, 2010

degree of transparency is hard to emulate. It was riveting and powerful. Real greatness captures the art of being true to oneself, of having nothing to prove and therefore nothing to defend; and freedom from self-absorption and self-importance.

Humility is a value highly prized in the kingdom, doubtless because we find it in God Himself. He esteems those who are willing to bring themselves (or are brought) low, who recognise their own poverty of spirit, because He stoops down to our level in His desire to reach us and lift us to where He is.[63]

> *[God in Christ] made himself nothing, taking the very nature of a servant, being made in human likeness. And being found in appearance as a man, he humbled himself and became obedient to death – even death on a cross!* [64]

He is indeed the crucified, risen and exalted One!

He responds to simple faith, like that expressed in these children's prayers (verbatim).[65]

> Dear God thank You For makeing the world. Pleas make purpil team First so I and ure team can have a prize. Sorry For doing the rong thing. Amen

---

> Dear God, I love You and I hope You love me to. Cool.

> Heavenly Father thankYou For You overparing love. ThankYou For the miracles You have done. Tonight please hear my pray. Amen

---

> Dear God, thanks For giving me a loving Family and a nice life. Thank You For being so generous because You made the world For all of us and died For our sins.

---

63 2 Samuel 22:36, cf. Psalm 18:35

64 Philippians 2:7-8

65 Sunday School prayers from Oasis Church, London (2011). Used with permission.

Dear God. You are amazing and I worship You. Thank You that You love me. Please forgive all my sins and help me to be a better person for You. Amen

My heart is not proud, O LORD, my eyes are not haughty; I do not concern myself with great matters or things too wonderful for me. But I have stilled and quietened my soul; like a weaned child with its mother, like a weaned child is my soul within me.[66]

Young children set us an example of profound trustfulness. This may be because, by and large, they are very forgiving, don't tend to hold grudges, say it as it is and quickly move on to the next thing.

When told that her beloved granddad Poola had died, four-year-old Téja was troubled.

"Where has he gone?"

"Poola is in heaven with God," she was told.

Her little face lit up. "Oh, so he's still here with me."

Dilemma solved.

Our inner 'child' seeks similar reassurances, and it is the child of the *heart* that the Lord Jesus seeks to awaken. For many, this aspect of our personality is rarely visited and barely acknowledged. It lies in fitful slumber to be woken by events that threaten or frighten us. We then revert to childhood patterns of behaviour until the psychological danger is past. Only the rare man or woman will admit, and live by, their true inner reality. It is hard for us to live this way, because it is an implied critique of a society that places ego, image, intellect and 'stuff' – externals – as markers of success, and sounds the death-knell to any stakes we may have in that world. As Punchinello found in Max Lucado's delightful tale 'You are Special', what other people think

[66] Psalm 131:1-2

about us only sticks if what they say matters to us. The more we trust God's love, the less we care about other people's 'stickers'.[67]

The things that often have greatest impact, longevity and matter most to us largely stem from our internal and relational connectedness to people and things. It is this connectedness of life that we are after in the quest for simplicity. It is the awareness that what I do as one individual affects others, locally and globally. My selfishness or greed represents an act of injustice in a world where people starve for lack of basic human rights. My £5 bargain may be made by someone in another part of the world who does not receive even that for stitching a hundred such items in deadly conditions.

Contemporary culture is confused. It is insanely attached to things, and curiously detached from meaningful connections with others. Having more 'stuff' has become a pathological illness that has left us hollow inside, lacking the substance of a true sense of value, purpose and meaning in life. The inner loneliness that results is deeply damaging. Richard Foster is right when he asserts that the lust for affluence in contemporary society is psychotic – completely out of touch with reality.[68] It is one way we compensate for our lack of inner security and peace.

An easy remedy is to de-clutter: remove the extraneous noise; give away what we no longer need, use or want; make space in our lives for the things and people that do matter. By not allowing things to possess us we free our souls to materially enjoy everything. In exchanging ownership for stewardship we honour the Creator God, who has entrusted us with all of life's benefits, to whom we will one day give account for their use or abuse.

Some of the more pricey toys we buy our children or grandchildren are discarded in no time at all for ragged and broken playthings, or the blanket they trail around the house as their companion and comforter. It is this attachment to familiar, loved items that we observe, and that overwhelms the crustiest of us! Such unbiased affection is deeply

---

[67] Max Lucado, *You are Special*, Candle Books, UK edition, 2005

[68] Richard Foster, *Celebration of Discipline*, revised edition, Hodder and Stoughton, 1989, 100

contagious and healing. It is the essential 'glue' between the generations in any culture or society, which is why its absence or suppression constitutes decisive grounds for society being accursed. The severest judgement is levelled by Christ at those who subject children to harm and abuse.[69] How can our society escape?

> *He will turn the hearts of the fathers to their children, and the hearts of the children to the fathers; or else I will come and strike the land with a curse.*[70]

The call to simplicity implies an orientation towards increasing dependence on God.

> *The LORD protects the simple-hearted.*[71]

This helps us defer to the wisdom that is higher than ours and uniquely God's, rather than the wisdom of this age, a totally different animal! Acquired by trial and error, this wisdom is only slowly internalised. It gives us tools to manage the whole of life intelligently and sensibly, and do it well. It is the Father's gift to those who will 'do life' His way. He makes ordinary people who make it their task to enquire of Him – such as the poor, bereaved, meek, merciful, bankrupt, seekers, persecuted, peacemakers of The Beatitudes – wise, and wise people stand out prominently among their peers.

It also draws us close to the heart of prophetic vision. Simplicity helps us to see through sham and pretence; as in Hans Christian Andersen's famous tale *The Emperor's New Clothes*, where a little child exposes blatant hypocrisy. We discern this, for example, in the deep-seated conflicts that plague modern Western society, the legacy of the arrogance of former colonising nations towards the (then) developing world. We sow the wind and reap the whirlwind.[72] God help us to learn from the lessons of history and not repeat them!

---

69 Luke 17:2
70 Malachi 4:6
71 Psalm 116:6
72 Hosea 8:7

Freedom

Freedom is a strange thing. In its absence the world feels oppressive. Once we possess it, we somehow long for the safety of the old regime.

Having reached the stile, with only two steps to clamber over, a sense of misgiving clutched at my insides. Stores of vitality and zest for exploring new dimensions of my world evaporated. In its wake, a shroud of tiredness settled on me as the gate took on the features of an invisible, impenetrable stone wall. Taking a deep breath, I slowly surveyed my surroundings to get a grip on what was happening.

In the distance above eye level towered the masts of fir, pine and evergreens. These provided a natural boundary to the meadow beyond my path where sheep grazed noiselessly. They hardly stirred at my intrusion, looking up briefly only to lower their thin woolly heads once more to the grass. To my left stretched a smooth, grey lake behind which prominent hills rose and fell sharply, cutting across the rough terrain pile like swathes of ribbon in subtle shades of gold, green and brown against a steel grey sky. In the middle of my path stood the rough wooden stile, with its iron bar and little step on either side. It seemed to mock me, refusing me permission to access the areas I wanted to explore. It met my gaze with a steely, defiant look, conveying the energy of personality.

Suddenly understanding came, like an unexpected breeze wafting a light mist of wisteria or honeysuckle from some far-off place. It was refreshing and charming. I breathed it in and as I did tight bands snapped, releasing the momentary tension. The censure came from inside of me, the voice of the authority figures that had shaped my life and invested hopes and dreams in the young, promising personality they did not want to lose. They had meant well, and she did not want to fail them. They were the sentinels who guarded her path with advice and counsel. But this girl had dreams of her own that would take her beyond the tried and tested ways. A wild energy would sweep her headlong into imaginary encounters and real-life, out-of-her-depth experiences. Then stability would return and with it ordinary assignments. She was spoilt for the ordinary. That was the thing.

The stone wall writhed in pain, anticipating defeat. Laughter coursed through the girl's body as she clumsily half-leapt over the stile, causing mayhem in the sheep enclosure as she landed all legs.

I leaned on the gate in silence as she picked herself up, still giggling and weakened with mirth. We faced each other now, the stile between us, bearing the weight of my discomfiture. This fresh-faced, eager-looking girl contrasted sharply with my serious, responsible, other-directed alter ego. It loved time-honoured things and frowned at frivolity and waste. It wanted to lecture now about others and selfishness and work. It wanted to maintain a discreet distance and observe strict boundaries. The stile continued to hold me, assuring me of support and understanding. But it was no use. The girl was me, and in all fairness I could not deprive her of life to maintain a miserable, dying corpse. Her face was still wreathed in smiles as her eyes met mine and held them in their gaze. There was a surprising strength and nobility quite out of keeping with the girl I saw, as if there were other hidden personalities within her to be discovered and befriended with time. Drawing myself to full height, I deliberately detached myself from the stile and stretched out a hand, which she caught and squeezed. She held on as I negotiated the one step and with ease climbed over the gate and on to the step on the other side. With a nervous little laugh I jumped the remaining foot or so and turned round.

I had come a long way. It was hard to follow the old tracks, there were so many. But from my new vantage point it looked like just another world to conquer. There are as many worlds within me as around me to explore. Down with the walls! On a sudden impulse I pushed hard on the iron bar now facing my left. The stile swung back in the direction from which I had come. No resistance whatever.

Pulling it towards me and securing the bar once more, it was clear, I mused, that going back was always easier than moving on.[73]

Imagine, if you will, the fastest racehorse that (some say) ever lived, and you have the story of Secretariat, hero of the June 9th, 1973 Belmont Stakes and winner of the three Triple Crown races. The film is truly stunning.

> *All that power. All that balance. All that heart. All that speed. Secretariat was ready to roll. And the margin kept widening, and widening, and widening. By mid-stretch the Big Red Horse was ahead by 28 lengths, with the margin to reach 31 lengths by the finish...*
>
> *If you were there, at Belmont Park, you saw Secretariat in living color. He was dark red, darker than his normal, bright, reddish-blond coat. With every muscle churning in full combustion, the horse darkened in color. His legs, you couldn't see them. Not even a blur. You could see his white-stockinged feet. Like a low trail of vapor. A white wisp of flying fog. And then it was over.*[74]

Each noble creature and species within its own habitat and reach has the same sublime propensity for motion and precipitation, Homo sapiens no less. We yearn to be free – indeed, we were created to be so. God has placed the desire for freedom within our hearts! He exults in it, bequeathing it to His sons and daughters for a day yet to be revealed. That day will release us from the limitations of ageing bodies, the corruption of sin and the hold of gravity, sickness and death, and release creation from its bondage to decay, brought into the glorious freedom of the children of God[75]. We will fly – if only metaphorically!

Freedom is also the profound, heart cry of oppressed peoples. Idealised for the nation of Israel (and by implication, for every exiled, landless and persecuted people) in a coming messianic age, there is intense longing for peace and security in the hearts of nations which

---

73 Florence Joseph © 2000

74 http://www.Secretariat.com/past-performances Writer Bill Doolittle. Used with permission

75 Romans 8:26

will only find ultimate fulfilment in that day when the Prince of Peace returns to establish global justice.

> *Every man will sit under his own vine and under his own fig-tree, and no-one will make them afraid.*[76]

Lord, let it come soon!

> *I run in the path of your commands, for you have set my heart free.*[77]

An older translation provides a clue to the manner in which this freedom comes:

> *...when thou shalt enlarge my heart.*[78]

Or again:

> *I will walk about in freedom, for I have sought out your precepts.*[79]

In both texts from Psalm 119, freedom is linked with obedience to, and application of, God's word in the vicissitudes of life. If we turn to the New Testament, Jesus made the same point to Jews who believed in Him:

> *If you hold to my teaching, you are really my disciples. Then you will know the truth, and the truth will set you free.*[80]

In other words, freedom is the liberty we experience as a result of walking in God's ways. In the words of Richard Brooks:

> *There is a beautiful paradox in the psalmist's words when he says, 'I will walk about in freedom.' When you are really bound, you think you are free. Yet to be really free is to be bound – not to sin, but to Christ, to be a blessed bond-slave of the Lord Jesus, whose service (unlike any other) is perfect freedom...*
>
> *James describes God's Word as 'the perfect law that gives freedom' (James 1:25), and so it is. We may be sure of this: God's*

---

[76] Micah 4:4-5
[77] Psalm 119:32
[78] Psalm 119:32 (KJV)
[79] Psalm 119:45
[80] John 8:32

Word defines true Christian liberty and freedom for us, its genuine nature, bounds and limits. We are free only when we move within that sphere ... Any desire to cast off the restraints of God's Word points back in the old direction of bondage, not in the new direction of freedom.[81]

Rather than relegating scripture to the confines of the narrow and delimiting, we should perhaps see it as a broad invitation to a life that is 'bigger on the inside than the outside', to misquote C.S. Lewis's Chronicles of Narnia, *The Last Battle.* Or to use another metaphor, it is like the menu for an exquisite banquet where you are invited to first eat the menu to partake of the meal! Think of Jesus' statement that so offended His followers that many of them left Him:

I tell you the truth, unless you can eat the flesh of the Son of Man and drink his blood, you have no life in you.[82]

The heart freedom that the Spirit of Jesus and God's word are pointing towards sublimates all our longings and desire for fulfilment and satisfaction, for beauty and glory, creativity and fruitfulness, touch and expression, for union and oneness. It is the freedom of dance, and of the song of the Lord sung over the redeemed and the whole of creation. It is the freedom of play, and of laughter that liberates the being from inside out and causes everything within earshot to rejoice with it. It is the freedom of rest, the intensive refreshment and renewal of spirits, souls and bodies that remain forever, eternally young in the Lord. It is the freedom of worship, as our total being becomes a skilled instrument perfectly attuned to, and at one with, the sounds and songs of heaven's hosts that forever adore the Lord of glory. We could go on! The best we can anticipate, experience or dream from the place of deep longing, or perceive from God's word, pales into insignificance compared with what God has for us as His children! We have only a hint of what is before us, and what heaven beckons us towards. One glimpse of this place, one taste is all it takes to spoil us for the ordinary:

---

81 Richard Brooks, Strings of Pearls, Aspects of God's Word in Psalm 119, Evangelical Press 1990, 60-61

82 John 6:53

> *All the things that have deeply possessed your soul have been but hints – tantalizing glimpses, promises never quite fulfilled, echoes that died away just as they caught your ear ... If I find in myself a desire which no experience in this world can satisfy, the most probable explanation is that I was made for another world ... Probably earthly pleasures were never meant to satisfy it, but only to arouse it, to suggest the real thing.*[83]

Our earthly pilgrimage, like a serial thriller, is the story of our personal Exodus from places of slavery into the freedoms of life in the kingdom of God. At each stage of the birthing process we have a choice: *how much of Him do I want?* It will cost us everything! It is His voice that calls us to life, laughing as we complain and argue, coaxing us out of our safe houses. It is all much bigger than we think, for God is calling us into the freedom that He is. And there is no one as free as God is! He calls each of us by name, and we intuitively know that it is He.[84] Our hearts are not naturally attuned to His frequency, and adjustments need to be made before our hearing is adequate to discern His voice aright. Even then, we would be wise to wear L-plates!

Listening

> *Be silent before me, you islands! Let the nations renew their strength!*[85]

We learn to listen best as we cultivate the art of stillness. The clamour of our soul intensifies the drag of everyday noises. We really do need to be weaned – from our mobile phones, satellite and cable TV, favourite radio stations, our eBook readers, music players and tablets – in order to tune out distractions and tune into the still, small voice of God in our hearts. For we are becoming deaf to the voices of the needy and the poor in society, to those of our children and our frail elderly, as we communicate without listening and hear without understanding. It is not the hearing of the ear but of the heart that we

---

[83] *MERE CHRISTIANITY* by CS Lewis © copyright CS Lewis Pte Ltd 1942, 1943, 1944, 1952. Used with permission.

[84] John 10:3,4

[85] Isaiah 41:1

address, and the need to nurture inner stillness for our own sake, the Lord's sake and the benefit of those around us.

Ours is an age that will not wait. Learning to 'still and quieten' our hearts when nothing will stop for us requires a commitment to living counter-culturally and to learning to 'waste time' with our Father. How do we do it? Robert Weston, a seasoned listener and modern-day Levite for the Lord, offers some helpful advice:

> *Our processed, packaged society has become too far removed from the rhythms and seasons of life. As one cow said to another, as she gazed at a lorry delivering Pasteurized, Sterilized, Skimmed and Long Life Milk: 'I didn't realize it was all so complicated!'*
>
> *When the stillness of the open spaces calms our minds and inspires our hearts, we will find it easier to enter more deeply into the stillness of eternity ... It is not that there is anything intrinsically mystical or more sacred about the countryside. Others may find just as much inspiration in an urban setting. The important thing is not so much the place itself but the fact of setting oneself at some distance from the normal routines and distractions of life. A sanctified corner of your home (or a corner of a cornfield for that matter) is all that is needed.*[86]

> Drop thy still dews of quietness
> Till all our strivings cease
> Take from our souls the strain and stress
> And let our ordered lives confess
> The beauty of Thy peace.[87]

Busy, as well as quiet moments, are sanctified by the Lord, but how necessary it is to stop and depress the pause-button! In so doing, we acknowledge that we live *unto God.* Life, Jesus said, is more important

---

[86] Robert Weston, *Intimacy and Eternity*, New Wine Press, 1998, 50-51. Used with permission.

[87] Stanza taken from the hymn: *Dear Lord and Father of mankind.* Words: John Whittier, 1872. Music: Frederick Maker, 1887. Public domain.

than food.[88] If we understand that God is committed to upholding all creaturely life, we will treasure these times of stillness. He understands better than any of us how internal worries and fears eat away at our peace and sanity.

Icons may help some in their quest for a still centre, as they concentrate on a candle's flame or some significant object to focus the heart before God. Quieting the soul is like training a dog to heel: it takes repetition and insistence!

Another listener I know heard a tiny bird singing a song that was barely perceptible. The song of the little bird symbolised the sounds of loneliness and need emerging from the deep places of the heart that needed to be heard, and acknowledged. Our coping mechanisms are strongly designed to stifle such cries. Stillness helps us to hear, hold and embrace the broken parts of us that need to be brought to the shepherd of our soul for mending. He is the God of the broken wing who made us for flight and freedom.

Lord, You love to speak
Even without the need for words
You listen to our inmost thoughts
And bring us to a place of stillness.
Guard our hearing –
For listening is the gateway
To the intimate communion
That both we and You
Are longing for.[89]

The spirituality of stillness and silence will be irksome for some individuals and personality types. It is worth keeping our goal in view: to tune into the 'here and now' of the present moment to discern our Father's voice. He rarely shouts. He won't compete with the other

88 Luke 12:23
89 Robert Weston. Poem used with the full permission of Ruach Breath of Life Ministries.

voices directing our gaze this way and that. He is the waiting God who teaches us the art – and benefits – of waiting on Him.

It is the spirituality of the desert.

> *Nothing happens fast in the heat of the desert. There is a different understanding of time, and it involves a lot of waiting. A world addicted to ever faster ways of doing things finds such a place deeply frustrating – a waste of time, in fact.*
>
> *The story goes that a desert father was visited by three men who wanted to talk to him. He showed them to a nearby cave and offered them hospitality and then left them there – for three years – before going to see what they wanted!*
>
> *The desert weans us off our addiction to the instant, the immediate. Spiritual maturity requires a quite different sense of time. We are not an age that can come to this truth easily.*[90]

Waiting for God is not to be compared with Samuel Beckett's famous play *Waiting for Godot*, who never shows up.

> *Listen! My lover! Look! Here he comes, leaping across the mountains, bounding over the hills.*[91]

His voice is life to waiting, hungry hearts. In the words of the well-known hymn:

> He speaks, and listening to His voice,
> New life the dead receive.
> The mournful, broken hearts rejoice;
> The humble poor believe.[92]

> *When your words came, I ate them; they were my joy and my heart's delight, for I bear your name, O LORD God Almighty.*[93]

---

[90] David Runcorn, *Spirituality Workbook* (re-issue): A guide for explorers, pilgrims and seekers, SPCK, 2011, 12. Used by permission of SPCK

[91] Song of Songs 2:8

[92] Charles Wesley, *O for a thousand tongues to sing*, words written 1739

[93] Jeremiah 15:16

As Jeremiah the prophet found, this is a place few will venture with us in the early stages. It becomes, over time, a holy addiction to the presence of God that would seem wholly self-centred were it not for the power it imparts for effective service in the world. If the goal is intimacy, the fruit of such times spent with the Lord is uncommon favour with God and unusual openings to touch people's lives for Him.

As stillness leads to encounter with the Holy One, we may be surprised at what we hear. Bells may start to ring: an unresolved issue requiring immediate action, a priority need to bring before God, a warning alert. We may pick up things close to the Father's heart that have no direct relation to us. After a teenage boy's abduction from a London Underground station made headline news, a group of intercessors listened to the Father, were subsequently directed to a street address and, following a quiet reconnaissance trip, handed over the information anonymously to the police. The missing boy was never found, and prayer continued on-and-off for a number of years until the burden lifted. And in an unrelated incident one friend, sensing someone was in special need of deliverance, picked up an imaginary hand-bell in prayer and began ringing it furiously as if to broadcast an announcement of God's intervention in the situation!

> The Bell of Creation is ringing forever
> And all of the while it is coming to be
> The Bell of Creation is ringing forever
> And all of the while it is ringing in me
> Ring Bell over the land
> Ring Bell under the sea
> The Bell of Creation is ringing forever
> And all of the while it is ringing in me![94]

There is a deep, satisfying well to drink from in the place of the stilled heart. Willingness to invest time in the pursuit of God pays such rich dividends, one wonders at the reluctance of the mainstream church

[94] Author unknown

today to rediscover and unblock the wells previous generations have dug. To the ancient paths!

Hunger

> *Is not this the kind of fasting I have chosen: to loose the chains of injustice and untie the cords of the yoke, to set the oppressed free and break every yoke? Is it not to share your food with the hungry and to provide the poor wanderer with shelter – when you see the naked, to clothe him, and not to turn away from your own flesh and blood?*[95]

Images of starving or dying children are so commonplace they hardly shock us anymore. The metaphor of hunger is therefore an elusive one. We really don't know what 'hungry' looks like close up. To cite just one statistic, sixty-five per cent of the world's hungry live in only seven countries: India, China, the Democratic Republic of Congo, Bangladesh, Indonesia, Pakistan and Ethiopia.[96] In this sense, hunger refers to the want or scarcity of food, and the discomfort, craving appetite, weakness and exhausted condition such malnutrition induces. The other sense in which the word is used is to describe strong desire or craving, which we refer to here.

Hunger and thirst are twinned in Psalm 107:

> *They were hungry and thirsty, and their lives ebbed away. Then they cried out to the Lord in their trouble, and he delivered them ... he satisfies the thirsty and fills the hungry with good things. He turned the desert into pools of water ... there he brought the hungry to live.*[97]

Elsewhere in the Psalms 'the hungry' represents the poor.

> *He upholds the cause of the oppressed and gives food to the hungry.*[98]

---

[95] Isaiah 58:6-7

[96] Source: Food and Agriculture Organization of the United Nations, 2010: *http://www.wfp.org/hunger/stats*

[97] Psalm 107:5-6,8-9,35-36

[98] Psalm 146:7

Such generosity of heart was proof of individual righteousness by covenant standards (cf. Ezekiel 18:16). Jesus Himself made the link between physical and spiritual hunger, and its satisfaction in God.

> *Blessed are those who hunger and thirst for righteousness, for they will be filled.*[99]

The coming of God's kingdom in Messiah was prophesied as the reversal of all injustices:

> *He has filled the hungry with good things but has sent the rich away empty.*[100]

Jesus, finally, declared that the hungry and thirsty would be fully satisfied as they put their faith in Him.

> *I am the bread of life. He who comes to me will never go hungry, and he who believes in me will never be thirsty.*[101]

Just as God's anger is a permanent feature of His judgement against the powers of dispossession and oppression, so mercy and loving-kindness are the permanent state of His heart towards the powerless and the weak.

The hungry, then, are a type of the spiritually bankrupt of any age or disposition. This is how enlargement of heart begins: with a sense of abject poverty, compelling need and deep desire for God. This kind of hunger cannot be faked. It is not politically correct nor trendy. Rather, it is the stuff of which revival movements are born and fanned into flame; as this cry from the heart of the Prince of Preachers, Charles Haddon Spurgeon:

> *O God, send us the Holy Ghost! Give us both the breath of spiritual life and the fire of unconquerable zeal. O Thou art our God, answer us by fire, we pray Thee! Answer us both by wind and fire, and then we shall see Thee to be God indeed. The kingdom comes not, and the work is flagging. Oh, that Thou wouldst send the wind and the fire! Thou wilt do this when we*

---

[99] Matthew 5:6
[100] Luke 1:53
[101] John 6:35

are all of one accord, all believing, all expecting, all prepared by prayer.

Lord, bring us to this waiting state! God, send us a season of glorious disorder. Oh, for a sweep of the wind that will set the seas in motion, and make our ironclad brethren, now lying so quietly at anchor, to roll from stem to stern!

Oh, for the fire to fall again – fire which shall affect the most stolid! Oh, that such fire might first sit upon the disciples, and then fall on all around! O God, Thou art ready to work with us today even as Thou didst then. Stay not, we beseech Thee, but work at once.

Break down every barrier that hinders the incoming of Thy might! Give us now both hearts of flame and tongues of fire to preach Thy reconciling word, For Jesus' sake! Amen! [102]

It speaks, in part, of a holy dissatisfaction with the status quo, coupled with an inner restlessness born of impatience at the slow pace of change, and the overwhelming conviction that there is much more to be experienced in God. There is *always* more! It seems that desire for God is related to a sense of lack, in the same way that hope is related to what we do not yet have.[103] It was not always so; the first Adam experienced unbroken fellowship with the Father until 'the fall'. We understand too that in the messianic age to come, the new heavens and new earth will obliterate the former order of sorrow, injustice and pain. So it is here, in the realm of the 'now and the not yet' that we have opportunity to enlarge our capacity for, and press into, more of God. To what end?

It's about *the* wedding of the century. The focus of biblical history and prophecy culminates in a marriage:

Come, I will show you the bride, the wife of the Lamb. [104]

---

[102] Cited by Robert H. Lecelius, *Spurgeon and Revival*, in Reformation & Revival, Volume 3, Number 2, Spring 1994, A Quarterly Journal for Church Leadership. Taken from *The Pentecostal Wind and Fire*, September 18, 1881

[103] Romans 8:25

[104] Revelation 21:9

As the bridegroom to his chosen,
As the king unto his realm,
As the keep unto the castle,
As the pilot to the helm,
So, Lord, art Thou to me.

As the fountain in the garden,
As the candle in the dark,
As the treasure in the coffer,
As the manna in the ark,
So, Lord, art Thou to me.

As the ruby in the setting,
As the honey in the comb,
As the light within the lantern,
As the father in the home,
So, Lord, art Thou to me.

As the sunshine in the heavens,
As the image in the glass,
As the fruits upon the fig tree,
As the dew upon the grass,
So, Lord, art Thou to me.[105]

We are to be married, no less. The final and finest of the prophetic heralds in scripture, John the Baptist, had this to say:

> *The bride belongs to the bridegroom. The friend who attends the bridegroom waits and listens for him, and is full of joy when he hears the bridegroom's voice. That joy is mine, and it is now complete.*[106]

---

[105] Johannes Tauler (1300-1361), translated by Emma Frances Shuttleworth Bevan, 1858. Public Domain

[106] John 3:29

Hunger for God is an expression of the growing fascination and delight of the bride with her divine Lover, as we, His Church, prepare ourselves individually and corporately to be with Him forever. It speaks of anticipation and longing for the wedding day. What bride does not get excited at the prospect?

It would be bizarre, would it not, if she waited until their nuptials to express her love in the most tender and intimate terms? Or did not spend all her time with the man she loves and will be living with for the rest of her life? God's promise to a deserted city was that "the sounds of joy and gladness, the voices of bride and bridegroom, and the voices of those who bring thank-offerings to the house of the LORD"[107] would once more be heard in her streets. Restoration gives hungry hearts something to celebrate, for God comes to satisfy, nourish and replenish the empty places of life. And He is coming again – this time to make an end of all suffering and to take away His lovers, worshippers and friends.

Amen. Come, Lord Jesus.

---

[107] Jeremiah 33:11

CHAPTER FOUR

Rest

Night

God called the light "day", and the darkness he called "night". And there was evening, and there was morning – the first day.[108]

The vision of the enlarged heart, which at least to some degree speaks in microcosmic terms of life to come in the future kingdom of God, would not be complete without exploring some of the processes God uses to create longing for the heavenly home. Left to ourselves we would settle for far less than God intends for us. The tough experiences of life create a certain internal tension and momentum designed to make us turn to God in dependence and faith, and yearn for release from suffering. The night therefore represents not only the hours of darkness between sunset and sunrise, but a particular season of the soul where, I believe, God seeks to silence inner noise and bring the heart into stillness and rest. It is a time of developing night vision, when our faculties are trained to respond to the voice of our Father when we cannot see Him or discern His presence with our heightened senses.

Let him who walks in the dark, who has no light, trust in the name of the LORD and rely on his God.[109]

Night is also a metaphor for periods of distress when the heart feels bereft of the comforting presence and guidance of God; for a time in

[108] Genesis 1:5
[109] Isaiah 50:10

history marking the unbridled reign of evil and the forces of darkness;[110] and for the alienation of humanity from God characterised by spiritual night.

> *You are all sons of the light and sons of the day. We do not belong to the night or to the darkness.[111]*

While the night lasts it can seem interminably long. Our sense of time gets skewed. Ten minutes can feel like three hours! Unless we are those happy souls that, once their head hits the pillow, are out 'like a light', we may feel ourselves spiralling into despair or bracing ourselves for an escalation of pain that is more manageable (or less noticeable) by day.

> I will hold the Christ light for you
> In the night-time of your fear
> I will hold my hand out to you
> Speak the peace you long to hear.[112]

The Son of God recognised that night heralded the completion of His life's work, then submitted Himself to His Father in total trust and acceptance of the cup He would drink after that.[113] Experiences of death, sickness and sudden loss of any kind may throw us into turmoil, requiring that we lean heavily on Christ's completed work in salvation and redemption and draw strength from His victory. At other times, entering His rest is voluntary. We learn to appropriate the goods of the kingdom purchased for us through the atoning work of the cross. Night is a necessary part of the cycle of times and seasons God has ordained in His wisdom. Only in the New Jerusalem will there be no more

---

[110] John 13:20

[111] 1 Thessalonians 5:5

[112] From *The Servant Song,* Richard Gillard © 1977 Universal Music – Brentwood Benson Publishing (adm CapitolCMGPublishing.com/UK/Eire Song Solutions *www.songsolutions.org*). All rights reserved. Used by permission.

[113] John 9:4

night.[114] So these times serve as part of our preparation for the glory that lies ahead.

Life was never easy for Sunil. He was diagnosed with dyspraxia, Asperger syndrome, epilepsy and Hodgkin's disease. However, he was seldom overcome by self-pity or a complaining spirit. Sunil considered himself "fit, fat and fine", though "well-padded" was his favourite description of himself. All that medication he was subjected to contributed to his being bloated more often than not. He loved laughter, his mother noted, and never allowed an opportunity to laugh to slip away. He could always find something humorous even in the worst of circumstances. He was one quick to say sorry.

Sunil had always been a people person. It was not difficult for him to make friends. He was generous with no concept of money. He had no concept of time. He would lose track of time. He could not tell the time in terms of minutes and hours.

Despite the insurmountable challenges he faced in going to school as a very sickly boy, he enjoyed art tremendously. He could be found in the art area during his many free moments. Art was one of Sunil's loves and passions. Since Sunil became very ill and was not able to go to school regularly, an art tutor was assigned to him. Jacqueline, the tutor, noticed that he possessed an extraordinary talent. They met on Tuesday mornings. She enjoyed listening to Sunil and looking at his beautiful drawings. Most of his sketches and drawings were full of animal images. Sunil's love of eagles was very evident in his paintings. The day before the Lord took him, aged17, he had fulfilled a four-year cherished dream to see the Stellar Sea eagles at close range when visiting the Birds of Prey Centre. He spied

---

[114] Revelation 21:25

them from his wheelchair. He learned the secret of their strength before taking his own flight home.[115]

Even youths grow tired and weary, and young men stumble and fall; but those who hope in the LORD will renew their strength. They will soar on wings like eagles; they will run and not grow weary, they will walk and not be faint.[116]

Such a surprising exchange of strength often comes at critical moments as a result of yielding to, not resisting, circumstances the Lord may allow in His sovereign purposes – the grace of relinquishment. It is ever His intention to break our obsessive need to control, in order to reveal the secrets of how His kingdom works and give us eagle-like vision, perspective and flight. His ways are frequently taught in the discipline of 'night' experiences when we learn to wait afresh on God.

Linda was driving along with Jesus in the passenger seat when the car began to accelerate of its own accord, eating up the road at increasing speed while she desperately tried to apply the brakes. The Lord looked at her, a gentle smile on His face. She got the message and somehow managed to stop the car. Swopping places, Linda let Him take over the steering wheel. She understood that God was speaking to her through the vision about relinquishing control and the fears that held her back so that He could speed things up in her life.[117]

Visions normally occur during waking hours when we are fully conscious, but dreams are the language of the night. The body's repose

[115] Text extracted from Florence TAN Poh Lian, Moving Moments With My Maker (in memory of Sunil Paul Thomas), pp5,7,11,14,17,23,27 ©2004. Used with permission.

[116] Isaiah 40:30-31

[117] Used with permission

in sleep is a signal for the unconscious to be awakened. The dreams of our hearts reside there, together with the unprocessed thoughts, memories and activities that fill our daily lives. These need expression. Some dreams result from the exertion of the day and some, doubtless, from the leftovers of the stomach! Others however are the deep, meaningful discourses of heart and spirit over which the Holy Spirit broods. It was in sleep that the patriarch Jacob saw a stairway reaching from earth to heaven, on which angels of God ascended and descended. The Sovereign Lord stood above it, releasing the destiny of a man and a nation.[118] The dream would be realised fully thousands of years later in the person of Messiah.[119] The nation would give birth to Jesus, the One through whom all nations would ultimately be blessed. In this powerful encounter, Jacob understood that the place where he slept was the house of God and the gate of heaven, a place of brokerage and revelation, and the pivotal point where heaven and earth met – where the gifts of the ascended Christ are released and appropriated.[120]

Dreams and visions are invitations to partner with our Father in creating new potentialities, and to receive gifts to enable them to happen. These may come in the form of ideas, projects, solutions, commissions, stirrings and impartation. The Holy Spirit's work is to plant these seeds within us, hovering over the 'deep' of our psyche until heaven's word of release comes, as He did over unorganised matter at the beginning of the Genesis narrative.

I slept but my heart was awake.[121]

The Lord often stirs people during the 'night watches', a time conducive for prayer, writing and thinking. Awake or asleep, our hearts can be attuned and sensitive to His voice. Just as a parent is roused by their child's restlessness, so the Lord keeps watch over His own.

---

[118] Genesis 28:12-15

[119] John 1:51

[120] Bill Johnson, *The supernatural power of a transformed mind,* Destiny Image Publishers, Inc., 2005, 58-62

[121] Song of Songs 5:2

He who watches over you will not slumber.[122]

He works while we rest. He calls us into His Sabbath-rest in order to release His works in and through us.

> *Sleep deprivation, voluntary or involuntary, causes the body to succumb to structural and psychological disorder. My immune system crashed during a time of prolonged stress, and I was unable to sleep for nine months. I learned to lie under my mosquito net as still as humanly possible with all my nerves jangling and jumping, until the morning. Working in a semi-comatose state, plied with medication and the occasional prescribed sleeping tablet when it got too unbearable, prayer and hours of enforced stillness got me through that medical crisis.*
>
> *Sound sleep allows the complex restorative systems of body and soul to generate repair while active life is shut down, and makes possible the life-saving interventions of medical science. It is God's gift to us. It provides boundaries that safeguard physical and psychological health when observed. Sleep redresses the balance after overwork and over-stimulation. It gives room for the unconscious and repressed parts of our psyche to be exercised and integrated. In sleep, God removed something from Adam he would later get back transformed.*
>
> *Sometimes, potential lies deep within us that requires the touch of God for it to be awakened. Don't strive. Rest – and let God work it out.*[123]

When sleep is elusive, rest is ultimately to be found in God Himself.

> *He who dwells in the shelter of the Most High will rest in the shadow of the Almighty.*[124]

The shadow of God's wing[125] is a picture of intimate protection as well as the secure, refreshing rest that loving fellowship with Him

---

[122] Psalm 121:3
[123] Florence Joseph, *Living Light Bible Reflections*, September-November 2009, ©Nationwide Christian Trust, Mulberry House, Chelmsford Road, High Ongar, Essex CM5 9NL. www.nationwidechristiantrust.com. Used with permission.
[124] Psalm 91:1
[125] cf. Psalm 17:8; 36:7

affords to those who will hide themselves beneath it.[126] The heart's great solace is the solace of His heart.

Dawn

> *My heart is steadfast, O God, my heart is steadfast; I will sing and make music. Awake, my soul! Awake, harp and lyre! I will awaken the dawn.*[127]

The Psalmist, in a tight corner and desperate for the Lord's intervention, roused his heart to worship. He had taken refuge in the shadow of His wings until disaster had passed.[128] The night of danger and distress would soon be over, as he anticipated the dawn of his deliverance. Elsewhere, the Sons of Korah had penned in the national song he might have sung:

> *God is within her, she will not fall; God will help her at break of day.*[129]

David had utter confidence that the God of the minutiae of life would fulfil every one of His purposes for him[130] and bring an end to his trouble. Selah!

Praise – especially in the dark hours – is a defiant, radical declaration of hope in the justice of God that will eradicate all enemies. Oppressed and Diaspora peoples throughout history have thus kept hope, spirituality and community alive in their hearts, through their music and songs. Public affirmation of God's goodness and greatness rarely fails to stoke the fire of faith in the believing heart that alone can extinguish fear and gloom. The heart, awakened and stimulated, finds emotional release in the whole-hearted devotion and worship characteristic of ardent lovers of the Lord that never fails to attract His attention and delight.

---

[126] C. F. Keil and F. Delitzch, *Biblical Commentary on the Old Testament*, Psalm 17:8-9, Public Domain.
[127] Psalm 57:7-8
[128] Psalm 57:1
[129] Psalm 46:5
[130] Psalm 46:2

Praise, then, is the appropriate response of the heart to the certainties of God in the uncertainties of life.

> *The LORD lives! Praise be to my Rock! Exalted be God my Saviour!* [131]

There is an endless song
Echoes in my soul
I hear the music ring

And though the storms may come
I am holding on
To the rock I cling

How can I keep from singing Your praise
How can I ever say enough
How amazing is Your love
How can I keep from shouting Your name
I know I am loved by the King
And it makes my heart want to sing

The dawn chorus provides a daily stimulus to awaken our hearts with song, for He is most worthy of praise! The culmination of our life's work and travail, the end to which all creation groans in eager anticipation, is the enjoyment of God Himself as the heart's great treasure, goal and reward;[132] man's chief end is to glorify God, and to

[131] Psalm 18:46
[132] Genesis 15:1, cf. Deuteronomy 10:9

enjoy Him forever.[133] God did not create us simply that He might enjoy us, but also that we might enjoy Him. This is no small thing. He is the One the heavens, even the highest heavens, cannot contain.[134] Our praise adds nothing to who God is, neither does worship fill up any emotional or psychological need on His part for affirmation or aggrandizement. Praise is the normal way we express the enjoyment of what we value – whether a sublime piece of music, or a succulent steak. In glorifying God, we express our utter satisfaction in the Greatest of all goods as we enjoy and partake of Him:

> *They feast in the abundance of your house; you give them drink from your river of delights.*[135]

And in the process of being worshipped, God communicates His presence and His goodness to us. Sam Storms argues his case provocatively:

> *The proposition I want to place before you is this: If you come to worship for any reason other than the joy and pleasure and satisfaction that are to be found in God, you dishonour Him. To put it in other words, worship is first and foremost a feasting on all that God is for us in Jesus. This is because God is most glorified in you when you are most satisfied in Him. Or again, you are His pleasure when He is your treasure. Which is to say that God's greatest delight is your delight in Him ... Worship is a feast in which God is the host, the cook, the waiter, and the meal itself.*[136]

Anticipation of the joy to come is, in part, what steadied the Lord Jesus as He approached His darkest hour.[137] It will also steady us in all

---

[133] The Westminster Shorter Catechism was completed in 1647 by the Westminster Assembly and continues to serve as part of the doctrinal standards of many Presbyterian churches

[134] 2 Chronicles 6:18

[135] Psalm 36:8

[136] Copied from *Pleasures Evermore, The Life-Changing Power of Enjoying God*, by Sam Storms, NavPress, Colorado Springs, copyright 2000, 210-211. Used by permission of NavPress – *www.navpress.com* All rights reserved.

[137] Hebrews 12:2

our watching and waiting as history moves inexorably towards its night.

> *See, darkness covers the earth and thick darkness is over the peoples, but the LORD rises upon you and his glory appears over you.*[138]

Praise precedes vision, and it is supremely the vision of the glorified Lord exalted now above the heavens, and soon to be exalted in all the earth,[139] that will enable us to keep our focus during times of testing and difficulty.

> *I wait for the LORD, my soul waits, and in his word I put my hope. My soul waits for the LORD more than watchmen wait for the morning, more than watchmen wait for the morning.*[140]

"It's Friday, but Sunday's coming." The scriptures are emphatic that we do not wait or hope in vain. Night precedes day, and darkness precedes dawn. Our light has already come in the person of Jesus Christ. But another day – the Day of the Lord – is dawning for the whole of creation. We may have advance notice of that special morning, if our hearts are prepared and our lamps are trimmed and filled with oil in readiness for the return of the King of Kings, our Bridegroom-Lover!

> *And we have the word of the prophets made more certain, and you will do well to pay attention to it, as to a light shining in a dark place, until the day dawns and the morning star rises in your hearts.*[141]

Joy

I fell first on an apple orchard. The neat rows, the sturdy boughs, small clusters of rotting debris under the weight of russet-green, full-sized orbs, perfectly shaped. Each row was set apart from its neighbour by an immaculate green lawn. I restrained myself from

---

138 Isaiah 60:2
139 Psalm 57:11
140 Psalm 130:5-6
141 2 Peter 1:19

taking my shoes off to feel its caress under my feet, like the thick pile of a luxury carpet. It was so perfectly green, African green. I drank in the green glory and the symmetry of the endless rows stretching far into the distance. The fruit was destined for the markets but here I was, gorging on the ripe array with not even a hint of apple in my mouth. I pressed on reluctantly, as the boughs waved their greetings and graciously acknowledged my unspoken praise.

The overgrown path led down a track which I zigzagged across hard-packed mud to avoid stumbling. The bank of tall grass and dense trees closing in on each side made my heart beat faster, while the dull sky stared at me, impassively. My pace quickened. Something of the fear of being trapped clutched at my insides. The gloom accompanied me into a dry ditch out of which I clambered without noticing the lightening skies.

To my left, erect and elegantly poised, stood tall, proud maize in the gentle breeze. To my right, stretched acres of golden barley like a Monet masterpiece – another carpet but not a soft, green spongy one. This one was rough textured, vibrant with life and the knowledge of its potential. The warm hue cradled my senses. I sang and danced and shouted. I was alone in all this extravagance, and nothing would hold me back from the sheer joy of it!

Having got my breath back, I continued along the narrow green velvet strip. Then I followed a tractor trail, the ground packed hard and high where heavy wheels had compressed the soil on either side. The noisy intrusion of the busy dual carriageway tried to hijack my happy thoughts but was denied access. Up and down, over the clumps, until the fields were left behind and silence filled the air again. Silence has volume. It is pregnant with meaning and symbolism. Silence speaks. It spoke to me now of the sanctity of ordinary moments lived fully and completely, of the grace that filled each Now with strength and beauty. I listened, grateful for the wisdom of that intimate moment.

I came full circle and found myself back in an orchard – this time, of Conference pears. The slender twigs groaned under their weight. Each of the fruit boasted size, colour and firmness. Every tree rippled with vigour and health. I wondered how they would feel stripped of their prize possessions. For the moment, each gloried in its abundance and waved with serene pride. This was their moment of joy. It was mine too. I felt as full and as pregnant as the ears of maize or barley. Gloriously full. I burst with fullness. How full is full? I asked myself. Can I be fuller than this? Elated and satisfied, my now shoeless feet and tired body sank into the green pile and I luxuriated for a long while as the shadows lengthened.[142]

> *His anger lasts only a moment, but his favour lasts a lifetime; weeping may remain for a night, but rejoicing comes in the morning.*[143]

Like drinking the most pure, sweet, cool, bubbling, life-giving and energising water from the deepest, oldest well, joy is a marvellous intoxicant that emanates from a world beyond ours. Its source is the eternal springs of God – a continuous outflow of the rich life and potent satisfaction found in the Godhead that is an expression of their mutual delight in each other. It is heaven's finest Champagne!

What will this inexpressible and glorious joy[144] look like? Perhaps the story Jesus recounted of the impromptu party thrown for the return of the Prodigal is a good indicator.

> *Quick! Bring the best robe and put it on him. Put a ring on his finger and sandals on his feet. Bring the fattened calf and kill it. Let's have a feast and celebrate. For this son of mine was dead and is alive again; he was lost and is found. So they began to celebrate.*[145]

---

[142] Florence Joseph ©2000
[143] Psalm 30:5
[144] 1 Peter 1:8
[145] Luke 15:22

It was all this dad could do to restrain his excitement and delight in conferring the highest possible honours on a son made good. What a picture of the mercy of God towards repentant sinners!

Lest we forget, we have made a similar journey to the distant country and walked away from home. There are things we can buy into in life that do not profit us in the long run, and cost us everything in the name of 'having fun'. The moral of this ultra-familiar story is that we are likely to make bad decisions when we turn our backs on the Father's house. For the Prodigal things just got worse.

> *After he had spent everything, there was a severe famine in that whole country, and he began to be in need.*[146]

Bad company and bad allegiances forced him eventually into slavery, and he hit rock-bottom. The young man had traded his entire family and cultural heritage for a short-lived fling. When we do not know who we are, we find that life knocks us about. For the first time in his experience, his sense of self and where he fit in society was displaced. This kind of disorientation and alienation exposes the void at the centre of life.

> *When he came to his senses, he said, 'How many of my father's hired men have food to spare, and here I am starving to death! I will set out and go back to my father and say to him: Father, I have sinned against heaven and against you. I am no longer worthy to be called your son; make me like one of your hired men.' So he got up and went to his father.*[147]

When our entire worldview is reduced to the next meal, drink, fix or contract we can forage, we have missed the whole point of our existence. We have been duped. The turning point – the Prodigal's decision to go home – marked a return to sanity that opened up his real wound: he was dead to his dad's love for him and all that love contained. His inheritance was more than mere cash. It was his father's vast estate with its resources, status, associations, privileges, assets, recognition, responsibilities, joys, honours and future prospects with

[146] Luke 15:14
[147] Luke 15:17

all his father's affection, pride, esteem and love thrown in for good measure!

> *You have made known to me the path of life; you will fill me with joy in your presence, with eternal pleasures at your right hand.*[148]

Surrounded by your glory
What will my heart feel?
Will I dance for you Jesus?
Or in awe of you be still?
Will I stand in your presence?
Or to my knees will I fall?
Will I sing hallelujah?
Will I be able to speak at all?
I can only imagine.
I can only imagine.[149]

This, according to the Psalmist, is what we were made for, and what is captured throughout biblical literature in the imagery of wine and singing, laughter and dance, food and abundance. There is more joy to be had in the immediate presence of God than in the happiest and wildest celebrations we can envisage! The conditional phrase we dare not miss, however, is that this joy is ours in as far as we have nurtured and walked in the path of life that leads to the eternal home. As Richard Foster carefully articulates in the final chapter of *Celebration of Discipline*[150], genuine joy is the end result of transformation of our lives. Trouble and trials are part of the landscape of the turf that takes us heavenward.

---

[148] Psalm 16:11

[149] *I can only imagine*, Millard Bart, © 2002 Simpleville Music/Small Stone Media BV, Holland (Admin. by Songs Solutions Daybreak) www.songsolutions.org Used with permission

[150] Richard Foster, *Celebration of Discipline*, Hodder and Stoughton, Revised edition 1989

And the ransomed of the LORD will return. They will enter Zion with singing; everlasting joy will crown their heads. Gladness and joy will overtake them, and sorrow and sighing will flee away.[151]

Another powerful biblical metaphor for joy is harvest, the important season at the end of the growing period where crops from labour-intensive land cultivation were reaped and supplied bread, oil, wine and grain for next year's sowing. The Jewish calendar and feasts of Passover, Pentecost and Tabernacles revolved around the barley, wheat and fruit harvests.[152] Even if sowing was tough, and costly, harvest represented a time of joy and well-earned reward:

Those who sow in tears will reap with songs of joy. He who goes out weeping, carrying seed to sow, will return with songs of joy, carrying sheaves with him.[153]

The Lord Jesus used the analogy of harvest to speak of the end of the age[154] and the joy that sower and reaper alike would share as they worked together in the harvest field of the world.[155] The unpredictable climate of Israel meant that high-quality yields were not automatic. Each harvest depended on the successive blessing of God and, by implication, on the covenant obedience and faith that elicited His favour.

I will bless her with abundant provisions; her poor will I satisfy with food. I will clothe her priests with salvation, and her saints shall ever sing for joy.[156]

It would have been a time of festivity and generosity to the poor.

The shouts of joy over your ripened fruit and over your harvests have been stilled. Joy and gladness are taken away from the orchards; no-one sings or shouts in the vineyards; no-one treads out wine at the presses, for I have put an end to the shouting.[157]

---

[151] Isaiah 35:10
[152] *http://www.bible-history.com/isbe/H/HARVEST/*
[153] Psalm 126:5-6
[154] Matthew 13:30,39
[155] John 4:35-36
[156] Psalm 132:15
[157] Isaiah 16:9b-10

Exile spelt disaster for the land, as God scattered His people in judgement among the nations for their stubborn refusal to return. Yet it resulted in a purified and chastened nation He would restore to wholeness and a special place in His heart.

> *The LORD your God is with you, he is mighty to save. He will take great delight in you, he will quiet you with his love, he will rejoice over you with singing.*[158]

> *As a young man marries a maiden, so will your sons marry you; as a bridegroom rejoices over his bride, so will your God rejoice over you.*[159]

This introduces the wedding feast as a final picture of what joy might look like.

> *One day there will be the most amazing wedding celebration ever as the Church comes into her own. Blessed indeed 'are those who are invited to the wedding supper of the Lamb'! What's harder to get our heads around is that the wedding guests are also the bride – because this banquet is laid on for those who have believed in Christ down through the ages, who have held fast to the truth, often amid persecution. It's for the faithful who have believed, hoped and trusted even when things seemed very dark indeed.*[160]

> *Jesus spoke to them again in parables, saying: "The kingdom of heaven is like a king who prepared a wedding banquet for his son...*[161]

Imagine a contemporary wedding banquet, the months of planning and exquisite attention to detail.
Then, consider the guest list: the great and the good reaching back through history and civilisation as part of the company, and ordinary folk representing every known and unknown tribe and people. Add to that timeless music and palatial surroundings that defy any sense of being enclosed by space. And everybody present is someone you know

---

[158] Zephaniah 3:17
[159] Isaiah 62:5
[160] Christine Orme, *Inspiring Women Every Day*, September-October 2011, ©CWR 2011 Used with permission
[161] Matthew 22:1,2

personally or by association. That would be endless joy! Much of this picture reflects Western ideas and convention, but each culture has its localised equivalent of the wedding meal even as food speaks the universal language of friendship, family and belonging.

Cut glass, gleaming crystal, crisp white linen and silver service. The amazing flowers! I recall staggering into church one Saturday night with a colleague as we deposited the flowers from her son's society wedding – magnificent displays of breathtaking size and beauty on each side of the stage. And we haven't got to the food yet! All tastes have been catered for, sumptuous food from the four corners of the world, every kind of delicacy for every palate; fine wines and sweetmeats to be enjoyed at leisure.[162]

Similar to the way believers partake of Christ through the memorial meal of bread and wine until He comes again, the wedding feast speaks of the glorious consummation of the mystery of union between Christ and His bride, the Church, only partially explained in the New Testament. Marriage is a dim reflection and yet a marvellous pointer to this most holy of nuptials. Our joy will know no bounds! If gazing on the glory of the Lord has the present effect of removing veils of unbelief from our hearts and transforming us into His likeness[163], what then, when the fullness of His glory is revealed?

> *Whom have I in heaven but you? And earth has nothing I desire besides you. My flesh and my heart may fail, but God is the strength of my heart and my portion for ever.*[164]

---

[162] Florence Joseph, *Living Light Bible Reflections*, March-May 2007, ©Nationwide Christian Trust, Mulberry House, Chelmsford Road, High Ongar, Essex CM5 9NL. *www.nationwidechristiantrust.com.* Used with permission.

[163] 2 Corinthians 3:16,18

[164] Psalm 73:25-26

This is not the journey's end. We are on a journey that has no end. It does mark, however, a landmark transition – to knowing as fully as we are known.[165] Our destiny incorporates a continual feast of being satisfied with, by and in God. Forever and ever!

[165] 1 Corinthians 13:12

Related Books by the Publisher

Feasting on the Father

William L. Smith

The Bible is essentially a love story – a book that reveals the heart of a Father towards his children. God does not keep his distance from us, nor is it his desire to punish us. On the contrary, his love compelled him to send his only son into an imbalanced world – to suffer in our place, and to bring us back to the Father as royal sons. Now, we are welcome to the table of the King of Kings...

This book is an in-depth Bible study, centred on Song of Solomon chapter 2 and revealing the heart of a loving Father throughout the scriptures. Far from being academic theory, the teaching is a heart-to-heart talk and passionate exploration of how to enjoy God's intended relationship every moment of our lives.

The truths explained in this book have the power to change your life. Once you have feasted on the Father, you will not want to look back...

Songs in the Night

Adele Pilkington

Through her poetry, Adele Pilkington helps us to gain heaven's perspective of our life on earth. Although we walk through the 'night' of life's challenges, Adele offers us 'songs' of hope and glimpses of God's perfect plan behind every moment.